THE WISE MARIE

VOLUME I

By: Natasha Brune

WM

This book is a raw, unfiltered journey into the depths of a life touched by addiction, crime, and trauma, yet driven by an unyielding spirit of survival and transformation. Through vivid storytelling, the author doesn't shy away from the dark corners of reality, while also infusing hope and the promise that change is possible. Wise Marie's story is not just an account of struggles, but a testament to the power of perseverance, vision, and personal growth. A compelling read for those seeking an honest and intense exploration of life's harshest realities.

Peggy McColl, New York Times Best-Selling Author

Get ready for the ride of your life.

Wise Marie’s story is what legends are made of. From the moment we met this woman, we knew she was special. This is one kick-ass lady, and one can imagine the Caliber of Charlize Theron playing Marie.

When we first met Marie, we had no idea what she’d been through but from the moment we read the screenplay, we were taken for a rollercoaster ride.

Marie is a beautiful and strong woman. She’s what every woman will aspire to. In the screenplay based in the Pacific region, we quickly go into a flashback and find a young girl who faces many struggles and sold into a very creepy prostitution deal and slides further into drug addiction along the way. And what makes it even more unthinkable is that this version all takes place in the most beautiful and fantastic Paradise on Earth: Hawaii.

Like a beautifully woven opera, we see the rise of an amazing woman while uncovering the seedy underbelly of Hawaii and discover that nothing is as it seems. Like the classic noir piece of history - Chinatown - we will see multiple layers unfold and you won't believe it.

The first-time author, Natasha Brune, seemingly coming out of nowhere, will be a force to be reckoned with. Her book and her name will forever live on in the upper echelon of the best of literary luminaries.

Phillip B. Goldfine, Hollywood and Broadway Producer

What a story. Many times, some people hit a bump in the road and allow it to throw them off track. Read this story, and forget the bumps… see how this woman has plowed through mountains and never allowed anything to throw her off. This book is for anyone who wants to be entertained, learn about their inner strength, and wants to get stronger. You will truly learn that anything is possible.

Eldelmira Murrieta, Author

Sometimes, life doesn't just hit—it crashes down like a relentless storm. Staying in the same place, you're bound to get hit again and again. But what if you chose a new path, one that led to a deeper understanding of yourself and your true desires? In that shift, you find the strength to build unwavering resilience and ignite a powerful inner fire that propels you forward. Natasha Brune's remarkable book, The Wise Marie, is a beacon of hope and transformation. It offers a dazzling explosion of insights to overcome even the darkest of challenges—drug addiction, domestic abuse, and deep-seated trauma. Even if life's storms haven't reached you yet, The Wise Marie will spark countless aha moments and powerful revelations, guiding you to shape your life into a masterpiece. For me, The Wise Marie is an instant bestseller—a must-read for anyone committed to self-growth, awakening their potential, and ready for a kick-ass story that reads like a true Hollywood blockbuster.

Norman Gräter, Multi Award Winning Motivational Speaker, C-Level Consultant and Success Book Author

When it comes to this story, all I can say is, Wow. Wise Marie is a breathtaking development in the face of adversity. This story is an amazing journey about a strong woman, who strides out of the darkest reaches of her life and achieves greatness. Natasha's testimony is full of twists and turns that truly showcase that for anyone, anything is possible.

Rita Montalto, Author and Founder of 4 Pillars of Wealth Game

Wise Marie is a truly inspiring story that keeps you in stitches, whether from laughing, suspense, or tears. Marie's story is a heartfelt journey from underdog to shining star. I truly believe that Natasha Brune has cultivated a story that will show others how truly capable they are, regardless of their situation, to achieve greatness. I can't wait to read her future volumes and see Wise Marie on the screen. So powerful.

Kizzy Lee- Singer/Songwriter, Editor and Screenplay Writer

Trigger Warning

This book contains explicit content that may be distressing for some readers. Topics covered include drug use, substance abuse, sexual assault (rape), and criminal activity. These themes are portrayed in a raw and unfiltered manner as part of the narrative, which may evoke strong emotional reactions.

Please proceed with caution if these subjects are personally triggering. Your mental and emotional well-being is important—consider pausing or seeking support if needed while engaging with this material.

Disclaimer

This book is a work of nonfiction based on real events. However, to protect the privacy and safety of individuals involved, names, identifying details, and locations have been changed. Any resemblance to actual persons, living or deceased, or specific places is coincidental.

The book addresses sensitive topics such as drug use, substance abuse, sexual assault (rape), and criminal activity. These events are depicted for the purpose of raising awareness and providing insight into the realities of these issues. The author does not endorse or condone any illegal or harmful behavior described. Readers are encouraged to seek professional help if they are affected by any of the subjects discussed.

ABOUT THE AUTHOR

Natasha Brune is the daughter of a deceased published author and former advisor to the general in Vietnam. She enjoys a strong marriage and spends a significant amount of time in Colorado with her family and pets. They often travel to the mountains, where she finds solitude to write and create, miles away from any other humans.

Natasha and her husband own nearly $8 million in real estate, all self-managed and developed. She is a real estate investor and the owner of three individual LLCs, as well as a non-profit organization. She spends most of her time working in the relocation area of the real estate industry, trading her time for money in a dangerous, challenging, and mixed demographic arena. It is her wish to take her 92-year-old mother to destinations she has not yet seen, while she is still able to travel.

Natasha graduated with a 4.0 GPA from Heald College in 2003 and has been self-employed since 2015. She started her professional career in 2000, immediately after completing a three-and-a-half-year residential drug rehabilitation program, following half a year in a local prison. She was awarded a pardon in 2018.

She has won awards, been featured in articles, and has spoken publicly and professionally. She feeds her soul by giving back to nonprofit organizations.

TABLE OF CONTENTS

About the Author 7

Preface........ 10

Dedication........ 12

Prologue: The Conception 14

Chapter 1: A Strong Memory 21

Chapter 2: Instant Woman—Add Water, Baking Soda, and Dope 31

Chapter 3: The Syndicate Connection 40

Chapter 4: Rollercoaster Ride of Relationships—Far from Disneyland 46

Chapter 5: John, the Waiter, and Hiroshi San........ 50

Chapter 6: Back to Dad's........ 69

Chapter 7: The Gangster and My Love for Jersey........ 73

Chapter 8: The Devil Incarnate and Father of the Korn 81

Chapter 9: Child Protective Services 97

Chapter 10: Meth, Meth, and More Meth, Pretty Please 129

Chapter 11: Public Storage and Friendamies Galore........ 153

Chapter 12: The Good Brother and SWAT Team Sally 173

Chapter 13: Daytop Village, a Place of Change 196

Chapter 14: The PI, Summa Cum Laude, and Real Estate 210

Chapter 15: The Resignation to the 2nd Devil Incarnate........ 217

Chapter 16: Cook Street and a Weekend with Bob Proctor........ 222

Excerpts from Volume II 229

A Note from the Author 231

Glossary of Characters 235

Acknowledgments 241

PREFACE

This book is the first in its series to go into the mind of a superhuman with ADHD who is alive today to tell these tales. There are dark moments and there is comedy and tons of drama, or as I like to call it, a Dramedy. It is loosely based on the events in the life of my alter ego, Wise Marie. She is a gangster with scruples who morphs into her own persona to become who she was meant to be. She does not get to her destination overnight and it is only with the will and burning desire to be the image she sees in her mind that she pushes forward.

The series spans over decades of Marie's life. This first installment stops in 2015. Volume II begins in 2017 and will cover the entire pandemic and post life until 2023. The location is set in New York, both in the multiple boroughs of the city and upstate, as well as in areas of New Jersey, Vermont, and other states. Wise Marie is an Asian Italian American with two fathers, one Bushido Warrior mother, and tons of siblings.

There is sex, drugs, and violence. There are possible tears (both happy and sad) with graphic forms of abuse that should be rated for mature audiences only. The essence of these stories will resonate, deter, and excite—at least that is the hope and intention.

Like Wise Marie, if YOU have the burning desire and if you DO THINGS in a certain way, YOU will get WHAT YOU want, I promise. All these beliefs worked. I am living proof to tell the tale. The spirit of the book is to be raw, real, and supply the "Anything is Possible" (AIP) Vibe. This sentiment is not an urban legend; it is true. The imagination runs wild and raises the level of visioneering, which leads you to that with which you are in harmony. Gratitude and changing your old paradigms will pave the path to your destination.

DEDICATION

This book is dedicated to the souls who have experienced similar events—good, bad, or indifferent. May this be an inspiration, provide laughs, and be the Shepherd with the lamp across the field of life. To those who didn't make it out, may you rest at peace, and may those black roses be in the throats of the killers. To the hamster wheel riders, there is a door that unlatches from the inside. I promise.

To the Children of the Korn. At the time the book began, during the pandemic, I had a heartfelt paragraph written for all of you. In late 2023, when I had the need or courage to pick it up again, this is what is now written. May God bless you and your endeavors. It was and is your choice and path.

To my husband, I love you for being YOU and always being the balancing act of this family on both sides.

Bob Proctor, you changed my life FOREVER. I love you as a father, mentor, and guide. I met you ONCE. Who would have thought?

I love my two sons, who are not made of the Korn.

To my animals, only Wagyu for all of you.

To my assistant, thank you for being able to keep up with the speed of it all and remain calm.

This statement below I left in the book as it was written after a month into the Covid-19 global lockdown. Life appeared grim then, but it seems appropriate now as well:

The pandemic, post pandemic, and current times…May God be with US ALL and guide us to the light.

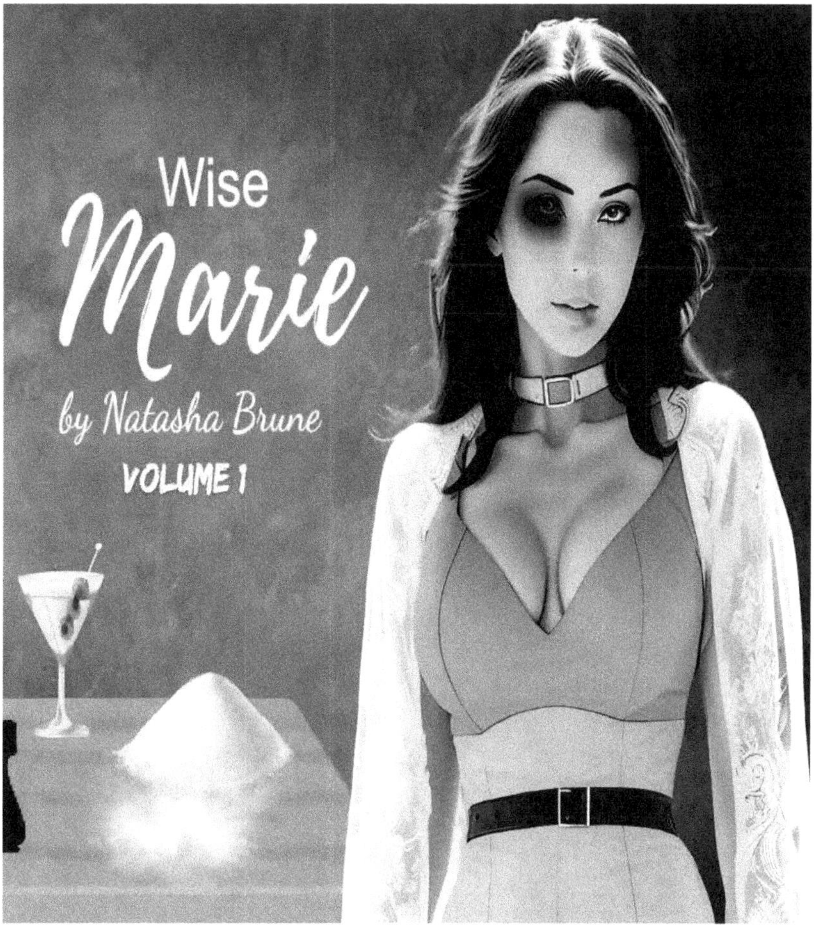
Wise
Marie
by Natasha Brune
VOLUME 1

PROLOGUE: THE CONCEPTION

I suppose in the summer of '69 is when she conceived at the Bachelors Officer Quarters on base. There was much talk around Fort Bragg, North Carolina, of a convertible and picking him up when he would return from tours in Vietnam, but we will never know what truly happened. We heard that it was one night. Life has a way of circling back like anything else, or as we like to say, "shit floats" eventually. He was, after all, the U.S. Advisor to the General of South Vietnam—essentially, a badass special forces army ranger ordered to merc over seven million people.

She was captivated by him—an Italian military officer from Queens, New York, with descendants from Sicily who had fled due to his father's career. He was a true Italian immigrant who sailed with others to find peace and live the American dream. His father was the chief of staff at the hospital and was forced to be compliant with the Calabrian 'Ndrangheta during his years as the surgeon. He removed many bullet casings and was paid to keep his mouth shut to the *polizia*. He left an estate belonging to the family for centuries that overlooked the Tyrrhenian Sea and abandoned most of the family's belongings, other than some important keepsakes. They needed a new start in a continent far away from the Cosa Nostra. She understood the immigrant part, to an extent.

She had grown up in an immigrant family that had moved from Fukui, Japan, to a small town in Portugal. She rode horses with her father and worked as a young maid for the wealthiest person in the neighborhood. She spent half her week observing how the upper class lived, and the other half dreaming of having her own house with servants, drinking tea and eating cookies on the veranda. Her brothers fished, swam, and forced toads and frogs to smoke cigars while they hid and drank. Her sisters were shy and stayed home due to their Japanese culture of "obey and pretend you're invisible."

Girls were to listen to their elders, work hard, and be humble. But that wasn't her style.

She preferred to tag along with her papa and be taught how to survive in the wilderness by paying attention to even the smallest of details. They were a funny pair—she talked too much, and her father was silent most of the time. Hawaii sent for workers from Japan, Portugal, and the Philippines. This group of mixed bag demographics was designated as the plantation workers and supervisors in the sugar cane and pineapple fields. They were granted U.S. citizenship in lieu of work and were awarded cottages based on rank.

She thought of her own mother, who for years, spent most days cooking and cleaning the physician's home. In those days, the milkman was truly a male. He drove a dairy truck and delivered milk to families. Mama would allow this man into the home while Papa was out. Soon, this man was familiar with the rest of the house and eventually the master bedroom that contained two beds. We do not speak of this and disgrace our elders. This took place in the 1940s, when such things were only whispered about behind closed doors. Still, history has a tendency of repeating itself, doesn't it?

In 1956, she moved to Washington to train to become a nurse, but would find more than an education and career. The Russian was from Upstate New York and traveled across the country, so he wouldn't have to follow in his father's footsteps and work for the large corporation there. He was a free spirit who loved to see the world. As a blackjack dealer in Vegas, he befriended people like Groucho Marx. He also owned a camera shop on a cruise ship. Wherever he was and whatever he was doing, the ladies loved him. He was blonde, with blue eyes and the longest eyelashes, but that wasn't it. He also had a sense of humor like Gene Wilder, which is who he would imagine to be as he would sing loudly in the shower. He actually started to resemble him in later years.

The Russian convinced her to work at his shop and become his assistant while she was in Washington. She was tired of the riffraff in Portugal and Hawaii and found it difficult to stay in one place. She also could not sit down long—known as the mischievous sister of the family (ADHD was unknown during this era). She loved talking and meeting people, and enjoyed the romance with the Russian, but still she went to school and would eventually become a licensed nurse.

While still attending school, the Russian proposed to her over the phone from onboard a ship from Thailand. She was just about to graduate and become a registered nurse at a local hospital full of polio patients, and she was excited to do her part to help them. But she was in love and love won out. She decided to abandon her career and move from Washington to the Bronx, New York. Tears streamed down her face thinking of the sick boy she left with polio at the hospital. She loved her work. She bathed, fed, and read stories to these children, but he stood out among them all. He called her Miss Yapi as he couldn't pronounce her last name, and she yapped all day long to him.

It was not long after that she and the Russian were married and with child in 1957. Over the years, she proceeded to have three more children with him. They resided in the Bronx, and her world was filled with constantly being moved from one address to another and then to another, from borough to borough, and then back to the Bronx. Rent to own, rent to live, and evictions with four children in tow, plus a dog. There was often one small piece of meat to feed seven people, with hardly any vegetables and tons of rice. She did what she could to provide for her children. Sometimes this meant one bag of French fries and tap water to feed five children and herself (always last). *Sad.* It wouldn't be a surprise if she was missing what she left behind. *The events that occur in our lives shape who we are, and in the '50s and '60s, a soon-to-be single mom was in the cards, and she knew that being chubby did not get you far in the world of a single, female parent who doesn't "count." She was a minority. And who the fuck came up with that word, anyway? Could the world be more distasteful?*

She was already shunned from her own family for marrying a white man in his fifties. She was supposed to be like June Cleaver. But this was anything but the famous sitcom from the 1950s. Her children were starving and so was she, while her husband was in the Blue Zebra room of a club taking photographs of the nude waitresses who longed to be models. He would trade drinks and other favors for complimentary portfolios. He would stay out all night, sleep for most of the day, and then wash, rinse, spin, repeat.

She would wait in the parking lot for at least two hours with the children, while he conned the owner of a bar to cash a check to cover his tab so he could then be paid in full and give a few dollars to her and the kids. A bag of fries for all of them surely had to be enough. She would pawn camera equipment and anything else she could find for fuel, rent, and utilities. This was the embarrassing hustle she had to do to feed her children.

Why didn't she just leave? Why didn't he? You didn't do that then. Better to stay miserable together than abandon your family. Better to drink yourself into oblivion, drive drunk with the kids in the vehicle, and risk everyone's life.

If a woman were not happy with her relationship or life in the '50s, then she would stuff her feelings and move on with her daily life until she died, especially if she was of Asian or minority descent. There is no such thing as a Japanese-Korean weakling. You must not be a disappointment to your family or friends. In present day we'd say, "Suck it up, buttercup." There was no therapy or prescriptions filled for people of her stature. There wasn't even an ear to listen, to take it seriously. You had to get up and survive. Tough shit was the answer.

Her dreams of a happily ever after became dreams of being able to feed her children and dog. This was no fairy tale. This was her reality, and she was heartbroken.

One night, the Russian took her to a party at a buddy's house, where she met Isabella, who she became very close to. Isabella didn't like the Russian, especially when her friend tried to hide her bruises and her tears. Those times, she hated him with a passion. Bella soon introduced her friend to her nephew, the Italian. And so it began…and went on for probably over a decade if one performed the math correctly. No one knew but those two.

I would later learn that the Italian's family consisted of an estranged wife, three daughters, and one son that he considered his sole and only child. To date, we have many who popped up on ancestry.com, and we have an occasional relative who pops up. Apparently, he was busy with more than just being a ranger. The Italian's wife, a beautiful Scandinavian, was hospitalized several times until it became her reality that the Russian mob was after her. They locked her up indefinitely and she lived the rest of her life sedated because of the fear of the Russians. Was she telling the truth? The family resided in a historic home in New York. They were Italians and the home was large, to accommodate booming personalities, activities, and the festivities that went on all year long. Underneath it all was abuse, and all the females in the family were made to feel like they were overweight and had to constantly be watchful of their figure. After all, it was the '50s and '60s, just like in the show, Mrs. M. She measured her waist every morning.

Still, a little girl was born in April 1970. Eight years after the supposed last child with the Russian. A mistake or accident is how she referred to this child. Someone had written to the Russian's parents to explain that the baby had black hair and looked nothing like the other four in the family, born as blondes, who coincidentally were all born on a Saturday. Weird, yet it is. This baby was the only one named by her mother and was born on Friday the 13th. They should have known then that there was going to be excitement. Buckle up, as we say…

CHAPTER 1: A STRONG MEMORY

Once, I read an article that there is a small percentage of the world's population with a gifted talent of long memory. I believe I am one of those people, at least part of the time. I'm just not sure it is always a gift. Sometimes, it's a curse.

Much of my childhood was spent in a two-bedroom, two-bathroom apartment, on the third floor of a building without the convenience of an elevator. This tiny space housed my two older brothers, two older sisters, me, and my mother, who had me in her late forties. The unit was furnished with the essentials you would expect—one futon couch, a folding mattress, four beds, and a tall credenza, complete with a fold-out desk that held encyclopedias and a series of *Peanuts* by Charles Schulz. Large fish tanks filled with exotic fish and eels sat beside Volkswagen parts and engines for my eldest brother, Peter—a gifted mechanic and marine life connoisseur.

My other sweet brother, Brad, was a great support. He was Peter's puppet, longing to be him one day, but his heart got in the way. He was timid and more of a follower. Peter, on the other hand, was selfish and a drug addict, bringing cocaine into our family. My mother, the nurse, worked a full-time job at a photo processing plant five days a week in Sant Antoni and was up before dawn and returned home long past sunset. Because we no longer owned a car, she had to take the bus to and from work. Sometimes, she would get lucky with a ride home from her co-worker, if she joined her for drinks at a local shady bar. So, Mom was always walking or taking the bus somewhere—errands, work, school, grocery shopping.

This was our normal without a father figure present in the home. However, the Russian did make frequent appearances in his Cadillac of the season, announcing his arrival by blowing the horn and holding it down obnoxiously. If we were down the street when he arrived, we could hear that horn. He did it to irritate Mom and embarrass her, I am sure, which I always thought was just awful after seeing her walk everywhere.

The Russian and Mom split up in 1970, about eight months after I was born. She left him while he was on a photo shoot. She planned this in advance because he was on the other side of the city, which meant it was a full day of shooting rolls of film and drunken debauchery. So, he would be home well after midnight, which usually led to Mom being slapped and thrown across the room.

After he left that morning, she sent my older brother off on his bike with strict instructions. He was to go to the school to get releases for him and my siblings (I wasn't in school yet). At the same time, she said to the others, "Pack only what you need and what you can carry on your own. We're leaving your dad and not coming back."

Then, she added, "Ever!" for extra emphasis.

She continued, "If you choose to stay, feel free, but I'm out of here."

My siblings all shook their heads simultaneously, thinking their life of starvation, drunken nights, and loud fighting was over.

Mom wasn't done yet though. "I'm splitting us up as follows. Peter, Kate, and Brad, you are to live with your Aunty Carissa and go to school in that district until further notice."

Everyone watched her, listening intently as to what would become of them—what would become of their family.

"I am going to live with Bessy in secret with Jennifer and Marie until I can save money for an apartment on my own."

I would learn later that Bessy was the Russian's former secretary who offered to help us. And so it was that we were no longer a family in that two-story house that was really never to be ours. We were homeless once again, but this time, we were also being ripped apart. We had to leave behind the few possessions we had—furniture, bikes, supplies, tools, linens, clothes, towels, kitchen goods, food (or what was left of it)—even the cute French Poodle and the car.

We reconvened as an actual family about a year and a half later, sometime in 1972, once Mom was able to afford her own place. A Chinese woman, who ran a tight ship as a sort of slumlord's paradise, was our new home. My siblings were all ten to thirteen years older than me, and with six of us total (including Mom), our new home was tight. Mom was in the master bedroom, one brother and sister were in the other bedroom with twin beds, my eldest sister Jennifer slept in the living room on a bed with me, and then my other brother had the couch, which meant the TV was always in his eyes. It was kind of appropriate, as he was the one who was always looking at the bright side of things.

The apartment had a back door that led you to a balcony that was connected to all the other balconies, so you could also use it as access to get out of the building—let's say if you were running from something or someone, like the cops. *Duly noted. Check!* The kitchen was separate from the living room and had one table with a basic gas stove, a refrigerator, and cabinets to house the very little food we had. The laundry area was downstairs in the garage where Peter worked on his engines day and night.

Growing up, Mom was a "hammer," or Bushido Warrior, I should say, given our heritage. She had a strict code of rules to keep all of us in line—or at least to try. Let's see, there were to be no calls during dinner, in the wee hours of the morning, or after bedtime. Of course, no one really listened. We just tried to find ways around it. In fact, my sister used her discount from her job as a telephone operator to buy a 100-foot cord to ease the pain of our social micro manager. When Mom's strict rules didn't work out well, she would try to make deals.

"If you clean the entire apartment, I'll let you go out with your friends," she would say often. So, I would clean until the apartment shined, but once I was done, she would not keep her word. She would say that she changed her mind. So, what would I do? Leave, of course! I remember once when I did that and came home the next morning, she hit me on my shoulder, cracking a thick wooden hanger on my collar bone and then slashing my arm near my elbow until it cut and bled. Do I think she meant it? *Yes!*

She said to me after, "Good for you!"

You see, I didn't experience the abuse that my siblings had. I was the mistake who came along much later. My poor brothers and sisters had it rough for many years. So, I guess it was my turn.

Mom was also obsessed with laundry, and let's not forget that the trash had to be taken out immediately once it was full, the bag replaced, and on and on. We had to wipe the entire laundry area with Lysol from top to bottom and the entire inside of the apartment. She ran our home like a prison, and understandably so. She had two boys who were handsome with attractive bodies and three girls who were equally as beautiful. The boys fucked every girl that came knocking. *Gross!*

She wanted to control what "types" of people we socialized with. You see, she is a Japanese-Korean who married a white man and dated only people outside her race. While this was not acceptable during those times, she did it anyway. Yet, she tried to stop us from doing the same. So, we rebelled just like her! The apple really doesn't fall far from the tree. It rings so true that we as humans tend to take on the characteristics of those that raised us. It cannot be avoided, and each generation tries to deny that they are like their parents. Okay, I digress. My point being that Mom was a complete control freak both inside and outside of that apartment, and she was also a hypocrite. It was her way or the highway, or as she would say, "Get the fuck out!"

Her OCD extended outside our walls though. When we went to someone else's house to eat, she would make us sit on newspaper. She treated us like pets that were visiting, so she wouldn't get embarrassed if we spilled anything. While it was a harsh way of raising us, it worked in some ways. And I am sure it wasn't easy to do as a parent, especially in those times. She had to be a ruthless, strong mama.

At home, our menu usually consisted of canned corned beef and cabbage or onions with lots of white rice. Sardines, canned tuna, Vienna sausage, spam, pasta sauce, noodles, saimin, and macaroni and cheese were other favorites. There were no fresh fruit and veggies, except the basics. If tofu was brought in, we got excited. Well, I did, anyway. I was a vegetarian in another life. My main meal was Ragu pasta sauce with noodles. I didn't care for the other items. I remember getting into trouble if I ate something that was supposed to have been a meal. I made my mother cry one night when she made canned salmon (this was a delicacy in her eyes) with canned tomato sauce and onion. She was so proud to serve it, and I about wanted to puke as soon as I smelled it. I tasted it anyway and gagged hard. It seemed so gross to have this fish almost literally swimming like a Cioppino in a can of tomato sauce and poured over white sticky rice! Well, I received the lecture of my life.

Jennifer had to be the mama for us, while Mom worked. We had no child support coming in from the Russian. They were tight times. All my brothers and sisters had to get jobs to support their own needs and wants, if there was anything left. They each started with a paper route. My sister Kate was embarrassed to go on her own and toss papers, so she dragged me along, lying that a cute boy wanted to share his chocolate chip ice cream with us to get me to come along. Somehow, though, he would never be home. I caught on after a while and then I just went with her because I felt bad.

The same went for everyone else, but somehow Peter always managed not to work. It didn't really matter anyway. When he did work, he spent all his money on himself, which usually meant drugs and girls. He never contributed for rent or food or any other essential. So, he used his only asset, his looks, to con his way into everyone's hearts. In some respects, I can't blame him. They all fell for it over and over again.

When it was time, Jennifer applied for full scholarships to colleges across the country. She managed to secure a 100% scholarship in the middle of Bum Fuck Egypt. Well, not really, but yes, in Duluth, Minnesota. She grew extremely tired of Mom's antics, gossiping, and the fact that she inherited all these kids to mother when she was a child herself. She didn't think that was fair and couldn't wait to get out of the house. Who could blame her? There was only one caveat—she would have to leave me behind. And what did that mean for me? I was being thrown to the wolves, as she knew Mom had no desire to raise a child in her forties on her income. Plus, it didn't fit into her new lifestyle. So, my other brothers and sisters would now be in charge of a very young girl. *What could possibly go wrong?*

When I was in the second grade, my mom started dating another white man. He was a sales guy who made a good salary. He gambled in Vegas once a month and she apparently knew him from the past. As for him, he seemed to want a loyal Asian companion to take care of him as he was twenty years her senior. He soon became my stepdad, but I was instructed from day one to call him "Uncle." I hated that "Uncle thing." It was respect, but why the fuck would I call my stepdad "Uncle," and how was I going to build a relationship with him that's normal? He wasn't my Uncle.

Mom started getting serious and going out to weeknight dinners as well as staying out on the weekends. She would bring me with her to these dates in the beginning, and I was uncomfortable. There was a night she took me with them to an eccentric restaurant with live monkeys. Yes, alive and swinging in the trees while you ate your food. Uncle was a big shot there and received VIP treatment. Mom drank too much, as was becoming the norm. On the way home, I was laying on her lap in the front seat of the car. It wasn't a restful sleep though, because she vomited her entire meal and all the drinks all over my thick hair.

When we got home, she managed to get me upstairs and then cleaned herself up, while I waited. But she just went to bed and told me she would deal with cleaning me up in the morning. I could not believe it! I had to lay down in my mother's barf. When my sister Kate came home from her night job, she was greeted with the awful stench in the house. She woke me up, took me to the bathroom and showered me, pulling all the barf out of my hair—one noodle and pea at a time. I'll never forget that night, choosing to remember how loved I felt by my sister rather than how abandoned I felt by my mother. I didn't care for Uncle, monkeys, or Mom for a long while.

It wasn't long after that Mom said I could stay home with whatever brother or sister was home that night instead of going out on her dates with her. This is where it all started going downhill fast. And as things progressed with Uncle, those nights turned into weekends when I would have to care for myself from Friday to Sunday morning around 9:00 a.m. I did a lot of experimenting in the kitchen with cooking, burning myself often in the process. What eight-year-old wouldn't? My brothers and sisters would pass through generally to shower or see what food we had, but they were usually loaded on dope. Sometimes, they would take me to their friend's house to get even more spun. It was there that I witnessed even more drinking and marijuana. By the time I was ten years old, I witnessed heavier substances in large white piles on top of dressers that they all snorted and pills that I would later find out were Quaaludes in foil that read either Rorer 714 or Lemmon 714. Of course, there was always a cold Heineken or Lowenbrau to wash it all down.

Mom made my brothers and sisters take me to school and pick me up. I would get packed on a skateboard and Brad would take me down the steep hill. I would jump off and land on my knees. I don't know why he could never figure out how to stop and get me off. I got packed on a ten-speed bike once and my foot went into the bar that holds the front tire. I had to be left in a driveway of a busy apartment building next door while Brad retrieved his tools to take it apart, then carry me up to the third floor until my sister Kate got home to save the day. Where was Mom? Working or with Uncle, probably.

There was some drama and violence while Peter lived with us. He had his own agenda and there was hell to pay if anyone got in the way. He was the cause of the first form of actual violence I witnessed. Yes, I saw him beating the shit out of his beautiful girlfriend, and he was abusive to Mom. He grew marijuana on the balcony, did drugs of all types, had tons of unprotected sex (his girlfriend later told me she got crabs from him) with girls who wiped their whorish lipstick on our white towels, and worked on cars until the sun came up with those ridiculous fish tanks that had expensive fish that we had to feed. I guess it was better to make sure the fish could eat than us. Mom finally kicked him out by calling the police to physically remove him from the apartment. *What did he do?* He moved down the same street to my sister's apartment that she was renting. By the time I was fourteen, it was just Brad and me in the home with Mom.

Jennifer moved away to college and was a lifeguard. I went there after my grandfather passed away and got to live with her for a while in her cool music store where I won a ten-speed bike in a contest. I met my first best friend who taught me to swim, ride a bike, and fish. Her mom was already running a bed and breakfast. She also had a tiny house trailer on the side of the house. This was the coolest family I ever met, and they had every bike model you could think of. I was devastated when my friend passed away from cancer at the age of twelve. And then, her mother, who chain-smoked, killed herself in the garage with the car engine running. The father and brothers survived. This was my first trauma of losing a friend.

I had another close friend in school, and we would have sleepovers at her house. Her dad owned a gun shop, where they sold all kinds of ammunition and guns. It was cool, as they had their apartment above the store. We played with the Ouija Board, which used to totally freak me out. Then, one day, this musician named John Lennon was shot by some psycho who just so happened to have purchased the gun from my friend's dad's store. It was all over the news. I never went back to her place again. I didn't realize how much of a big deal that rock star was back then. It was a moment to remember for sure. I believe her dad had to close his business because of that incident.

Kate was always working and had a social life. She would pick me up often and take me to work with her. I would wait in the break room and got to know all her co-workers. The point I am getting to is that my mother used her other children to take care of me while she either worked or played. On the upside (I guess)—we never got taken away by CPS and we were always clean and fed as much as we could be—at least not to be considered starving or malnourished. *Oh, the blessings we had!*

Brad was hardly ever home, as he worked, had a girlfriend, and was always out with Peter, which meant he had to stay away from the house because Peter was no longer welcome. I had the apartment to myself quite often and this was when I was going through puberty. I also started drinking and smoking marijuana. Why not? Everyone else around me was. And, of course, I made friends with those who had like-minded goals and agendas. Life was shaping up to be a path that soon became dangerous with too much freedom and no role models. It was a breeding ground for trouble. As they say, "Idle time is the Devil's Workshop." Truer words were never spoken.

CHAPTER 2: INSTANT WOMAN—ADD WATER, BAKING SODA, AND DOPE

It was the early 1980s. The music was great, fashion was bright, and we danced until our feet hurt. You could still roller skate on the street without getting banged by a car or raped by some pedophile. No cell phones—just schemes to meet at the park to smoke a joint or in some water tunnel alley up the street when we cut school. It was like the movie *Stand by Me*—every day.

We still lived in the same apartment and a huge storm was coming. They released us from middle school early, and of course, I had a stop to make an appearance in the graveyard to smoke some weed and fuck around before heading home. I never thought my mom would ever get sent home as her boss was a total douchebag with no soul, but I was wrong. I walked in and to my surprise, she stood there, glaring at me. She pulled me by my cheek into the kitchen and gave me the lecture of my life, as we were facing a hurricane. My friend, Ronda, and I stayed up all night long and talked while the wind was easily taking trees out of the ground. I fell asleep under the kitchen table and discovered in the morning that we had survived.

By this time, I had already started experimenting with Quaaludes, cocaine (both snorting and freebasing by this point), paper LSD, marijuana, and alcohol. I was having sex with my boyfriend in his mom's bathroom and behind a building in a makeshift clubhouse with a dirty mattress that he put a sheet over. And I got pregnant. It's probably no surprise given what I was surrounded with. No one had ever talked with me about the birds and bees, and definitely not about using protection. It was assumed that I should know what to do. How the hell would I know that?

I started gaining weight in the summer, and in my bikinis at the beach, it was pretty obvious, but not to me. My stomach started to swell, and I had larger tits that I wasn't born with and weird acne on my back! My brother Peter's girlfriend, Tiare, a Tahitian Goddess, was my only hope. You see, she was not far from my age. My brother was in his twenties at the time and living with my sister Kate down the street. But his girlfriend was only six years older than me, so she could relate. She told me that I had to tell my mom before it was too late, and I would not be eligible for a legal abortion. I refused and kept procrastinating.

So, finally, Tiare called my sister Kate and said, "Your sister is nearly four months pregnant and needs to have an abortion."

Kate had no choice but to make that call. She rang Mom and I was right there. Mom took the long telephone cord that we still had and beige push-button phone into the bedroom to talk. I heard her say, "No wonder she gained so much weight!"

You see, all of us girls were told by Mom from the time we were young, "Don't eat much! Take care of your skin and body because good skin, a good body, and a pretty face is all you need!"

So, that was Mom's take from the call saying her teenage daughter was pregnant! She came into the living room and told me that we had to schedule an appointment and take care of this matter ASAP. So, within days, I was in Queens to see her gynecologist. I received an abortion and was released on the same day. The first child taken away without my consent or input. It was as simple as—*End of story. No more drama or embarrassment to your family or friends. You don't have a say.*

I began rebelling even more, if that was possible. (It was.) I was going to nightclubs, stuffing my chest with toilet paper, wearing miniskirts that were actually tube tops, and putting on tons of red and pink lipstick with a glaze of shiny lip gloss that you could see from a mile away. That shouldn't attract the worst type of characters, right? I went to every rock and R&B concert that came to town. I hung out with the drug dealers, because that's the way to get the free drugs on a daily basis. I should know. My brother was one of them. He had the best white, blue pearl flake chunks that looked like they were carved out from a glacier. We had the best shit, and boy, did we think everyone was after us.

I also got closer to my dad during this time. I didn't get to know him well when I was growing up as my mom was overprotective of only me. She allowed all four other kids to go on trips with him to other parts of New York, and she would never let me go. Once when I was young, I had a bad accident at his apartment above the meat market plant. I received third degree burns from tripping over a cord when canned soup was being warmed up in his office/apartment, while my sister Jennifer was there cleaning and being his secretary. I shit my pants from the pain and was in the ER for hours receiving treatment for the burns. I missed a ton of school and mom banned me from being around him for months after that, as he was not demonstrating he could take care of me well in his care. He was also a drunk driver, so she didn't want me in the car with him. At the time, I didn't see why she was so protective of me with him.

So, I started to develop a relationship with him when I was a teenager, around when Mom considered me to be "incorrigible," as she put it. He stepped in to help me deal with life when I was becoming annoyed with Mom and her control freak, OCD, Asian ways of how she treated me (chores all day/night, never a moment to myself of peace, always negative, complaining, gossiping about people). There was never any encouragement and no help with homework. The only thing she paid attention to was if I dressed nice, looked pretty, used skincare, and took care of my body. For those things, she would praise me. Other than that, I was to cook, clean, and live on my own unsupervised, so the Russian stepped in with his style of flexibility and tried to be the good cop.

My brothers and dad were fortunate to belong to the IATSE Union that ran all the motion pictures back then. I went to my dad's. He was on set shooting all the time. We stayed in hotels and partied with the crew and actors. I remember going to a nightclub and Patrick Swayze was there—great dancer and even better body. We're talking movies like *Wall Street, When Harry Met Sally, Working Girl, Fatal Attraction, Scarface, Tootsie,* and more. It was exposure that could have been great if I had pursued my original goal to become an extra, model, and then possibly go into acting. That was my dream back then—use what Mom said was my best asset—my face and body (if I knew how to keep it skinny). *Priorities, people!* Did anyone say college or map out your goals? Yeah, right. I could not get help with homework, so I didn't do the work.

I met all kinds of actresses and nice set directors and then thought it was cool that my brothers were the ones setting up all the greens (plants) for the scene and Peter was craft service (beverage boy). We had tons of these photos of us with them. My dad and brothers were raking in high five figures, possibly more, which was good for only having to work part of the year. They would collect unemployment, as it's typical for the crew to be laid off in between seasons. They were living the dream, and I was happy to ride on their coattails because it meant more money, drugs, and fun experiences for me. Other teenagers my age were envious, and I could see why. I thought they were living the boring life, while I was riding high.

I continued to leave middle school without permission to walk to the beach where all the handsome surfers hung out. This was my favorite place because I could tan until I was a dark olive color and then walk home and see my mom for dinner. Repeat all week. I signed my own notes from Mom to my counselors and it finally caught up with me, of course. I was getting into trouble at school, hanging out with unsavory characters, and barely passing each class.

I would see guys whacking off on the way to school and it didn't even phase me. I was numb. One day, my cousin was with me when we saw a guy doing that. My cousin was so shaken up, she called the police. On the other hand, I was mostly worried about the ounce of weed I had on me. When I got called into the principal's office later that day, I was shaking, thinking I was about to be arrested. I gave my purse to a classmate and begged her to hold the goods until I was around again. But when I walked in, they showed me a book of potential whackers known in the hood. They all looked exactly the same—average looking men, medium build. One had a car seat in the back of a hatchback. I will never forget that. I did what I could and gave the description. I walked out and screamed down the hall that I was not going to lose all the weed I had in my bag! Score! Who cares that I saw a pedophile jacking off on the side of the road with a car seat in the vehicle, right? The weed was my priority. Yet my poor cousin probably has PTSD to this day over the incident.

To add insult to injury, my older sister Jennifer was a schoolteacher at my middle school at the same time. Talk about a bit of a conflict! Students used to get us confused because we had the same last name. They would write "Whore" on the wall and add her name—my sister, who never smoked a cigarette or joint in her whole life! She was horrified. I felt bad to an extent, but I didn't exactly have my priorities straight then, so I really couldn't give two fucks.

My sister would, of course, hear of the chaos I was causing on campus, and she refused to have me as a student, even though the other teachers begged her to take me. Apparently, I traumatized them. I was "incorrigible," as my mom put it. I ran away from home often. Finally, Mom called the cops, and I was arrested and put in the Girls Detention Center on Carpenter Avenue (which has since been condemned, becoming an affordable housing complex in the Bronx). I was also in group homes that I ran away from to smoke a doobie with my friend that lived down the street. I remember I asked to use the phone at the girl jail, and it was on the boy's side. The administrator on staff just said, "Okay, go ahead."

I walked into the room. The guard took one look at me and almost fell off his chair. I knew him from a few weeks back. We were snorting coke at Peter's place with his other older friends that had no business being with a young girl like me. We also met in a nightclub—another place I should not have been. So, what happened after finding my friend? Free cigarette breaks, special food, and treatment to use the phone—basically, so I wouldn't turn his ass in. By the way, I'm not a narc and would have never done it, but I played that fucker to the hilt because it sucked being in that place! It smelled of Pine-Sol and bleach everywhere, and we had to wear the same gaudy, itchy dress that gave me a rash.

Once I was set free, I continued down the same path with drugs and promiscuity. There was no deterring me—detention center or not. I remember trying a threesome at a Seaside Heights, New Jersey, beach with my cousin Tammy, who was a hooker in Jersey and lived in the ghetto (my home base from time to time) and this cute guy from Riverdale. I hated it. He loved it as he was getting two hot chicks in his car. Fucking pervert—he should have been shot as he was more than twice our age.

Another night, I went out and got super stoned with my friend John. He was gay, but we had a love affair. As he put it, "If I ever want to fuck a girl, it would be only you, Marie."

I was exactly what he wanted. He always said my skin smelled like roses. He was very sweet and it was kind of nice—or as nice as it could be since he was, in fact, gay. Somehow, I got home and fell asleep. By then, I was living with my sister Kate and was in charge of watching my niece, Erin, who was only about four years old at the time. Kate would let me smoke weed, get high, and bring guys over, and in return, I would watch my niece, cook, and clean the house.

Kate had to go to work early in the morning at the phone company, so I would be there for Erin. When I woke up in the morning, the first thing I saw was not my adorable niece, but a guy that looked strangely familiar to me (although I couldn't place him with all the gunk in my eyes from the night before). I felt him before I saw him. I had been sleeping on my sister's waterbed, and you could easily feel another person on the bed with you with that rolling raft motion, especially if that person was the size of a grown man.

I looked over at Erin and she was fast asleep next to the bed. The guy had his fucking clothes off, and I asked what he was doing there. His answer was, "Here to fuck you."

I screamed, jumped up, and ran out of the ground-floor apartment. I knocked on the resident manager's door, but there was no answer. Then I ran into the street, but of all mornings, no one was walking out there. I ran across the street and screamed, but no one came out. I hid behind the dumpster and had the driveway in view. I saw him come out alone with only his shorts on. He looked up and down the street and then took off toward the mountains. I ran back to the apartment where my niece was crying and rubbing her eyes.

"Why did you leave me, Aunty? Who was that strange man?"

I felt awful for her! I hugged her tight, locked the door, and called my sister, who called the cops and came home from work. We sat there for hours with the cops, answering all their questions. The cops ultimately found him and arrested him for attempted rape. I had to go to court, and it turned into a complete shit show. He received some jail time, and he had to register as a sex offender. Was it a coincidence that his sister bullied me a week prior at a nearby market and then my sister threatened to beat the fuck out of her? That's why he looked familiar. Then, magically, her older brother said he broke in to rape my sister. That was his story, so he didn't look like the pedophile in court—only a rapist. *Sick bastard.*

The court had a requirement to inform my sister of his release from prison each time, which went on for over twenty years. *I guess all we could do was hope that he got fucked in prison over and over until he got the worst hemorrhoids of his life.*

So, the night of that horrible incident, waking up to a stranger in my bed and being questioned by the cops all day, my cousin asked if I wanted to join her partying with the owner of a well-known tour bus company. I didn't think it was a good idea since all that had happened, and I was feeling traumatized. I didn't know then, as a young teenager, that I was experiencing PTSD. She said, "It'll be perfect to get out and forget about it!"

So, I went and snorted a bunch of coke and overdosed in front of the owner of the tour bus company, who was probably a married man that had kids at home. This would be scandalous. I woke up with Fiona on my lap, and I was drenched. My cousin poured a pitcher of ice water on me to snap me out of it. Apparently, I had had a drug-induced seizure. She was so freaked out and couldn't believe what she had witnessed. She didn't want her mom (my mother's sister) because she didn't want us to get in trouble. The loser owner of the company bailed, of course.

The last thing I remember prior to the seizure was him putting his hand down my pants and trying to kiss me. And me thinking that he looked like a big, fat, oily toad. *Another sick fuck.*

Have you got the picture yet? I was a know-it-all young girl with thick eyebrows, almond eyes, tan, nice body, face, smart mouth, no brains, drug addict, with an attitude that could kill.

CHAPTER 3: THE SYNDICATE CONNECTION

When I was fifteen, my brother Peter introduced me to a young Teamster, who was the grandson of Tony Mariani III. Teamsters and the International Alliance of Theatrical Stage Employees (IATSE) union guys all hung out together, comingling their drugs, parties, and girls. Tony's grandfather was a powerful man. He ran the Teamsters in a sort of secret location that gave off weird vibes. It was above a hotel and backed onto another weird building and into an older elevator with stairs. It was the secret building that smelled of cigarettes, cigars, and whiskey or scotch all the time. His son, Tony Mariani, Sr., was the president of the hotel union. They were the leaders of the two most powerful unions in New York. Together, they were the strong-arm empire in the state. Plus, they were close with the other Mafioso-connected union leader, John Fatone, the president of IATSE.

The Irish and the Italians were the strong arms behind the scenes. Peter thought Tony was more my age than other guys I had been out with, and he had money to spend on me. He was a young twenty-year-old that could play golf and had a sense of humor, tons of cool friends, a blue Volkswagen Rabbit that fit all his clubs, and most importantly, a library cassette tape collection of '80s music that was the best. I learned about the Psychedelic Furs, the Clash, the Stray Cats, Depeche Mode, and so many other great bands from him.

Tony was from the West Village—he grew up privileged, but also being exposed to seeing evil. He was told that he'd get whatever he wanted if he shut his mouth. He told me the same thing. Shut my fucking mouth if I saw anything awkward when at any of their houses. This could have been people, blood, unknown cars, weird meetings around the round table, drugs, or guns. It was so strange. This underworld life, but he had all the manners, practiced chivalry, and was educated and cultured. He knew how to wine and dine a girl. He also knew how to smoke and snort loads of coke and became the funder of our future bad habits.

We were having fun and I introduced him to my family. My dad already knew him and thought it was a good idea, as he was planning on investing into a generator business, and to haul the generators, you had to be a Teamster. So, this was working out perfectly for him, despite the fact that his young teenage daughter was with a notoriously crime-ridden family. What's that when he had his partner, Charles, send him money, and they both went into business providing the generators for all the motion pictures, commercials, concerts, and large events. Win-win, right?

Tony's grandfather had a badass house in Staten Island that looked unassuming from the outside. Tall hedges surrounded the entire property that included a pool and an apartment where Tony's sister lived, formerly the garage. His mom, cool as ever, Amy Carrera, was divorced from Tony's dad, Michael Aguado, and remarried to his stepdad Tommy Mottola, who could have been Tom Selleck's brother. They had a huge wooden cabin in the Catskill Mountains, lined with shelves of Faberge eggs from all over the world. I think it had snuff powder in them, but I digress. The bottom line was that they were all coke heads too. He was an actor trying to get ahead and she was the daughter of the Teamster president.

Tony's dad was also remarried to a nice woman named Debbie, who looked like she could be Mrs. Beaver. Tony lived in all the homes—in Staten Island, the West Village, the Catskills, and in upstate New York, where he hid for weeks on cocaine benders in the

Adirondack cabin by the lake where it was said that they sank people. He took me everywhere with him and I became part of this family.

He golfed and had me driving him around on every golf course and watching ever so quietly. He'd do nearly the entire course and then jump in the cart, snort a fat rail, and then lose his shit and quit the game right before the eighteenth hole. We would end up in the bar, snorting coke and drinking with the bartender.

Films were always being shot in the city. It was perfect, as it had everything you needed there, plus a nightclub or dive bar on every corner for more shenanigans. We had free bungalows or rooms that only the rich and famous stayed in. This was impressive for a girl from the ghetto or lower income hood. It was living the elevated lifestyle of the dark and dirty—as a teenager.

As Tony and I spent all his money from the movies on drugs, we started to lose what was in the kitty for a forthcoming apartment. Cocaine of the finest quality from Peru is expensive, you know. So, we had to look at his resources. He had an uncle who lived in a nice old neighborhood in the University Heights area who had several units he wanted to rent out in the same multi-plex house. Tony promised we would fix up the back unit for us, and his sister, Nicole, would move into the front, as she was the responsible type of addict, who could function with a job through the family, pay rent and utilities, and keep it straight. She dealt drugs too. So, we moved into this unfinished apartment that had no running water or working toilet yet. We had to fix it up, and while we were in the process, I remember having to take a shit in a five-gallon bucket lined with a grocery bag and told Tony that we needed to step it up and get a real latrine.

We worked on getting furniture and carpeting from the hotel where the Teamsters office was located and items from each of his parents' houses to make it a home. He got the toilet and shower working, plus the kitchen sink. It was a dump, but we made it nice. What did we do once we were all settled in? Freebase more coke, of course. I developed this weird paranoid tick of taking a big hit of freebase coke (crack), having it go straight to my brain like fire, and then in five seconds, blowing it out, thinking the DEA was at our door and ready to break it down! I would imagine the black shoes just visible through the crack under the door.

I would undress from all my clothes (yes, even the underwear), and be stark naked. Then, I would walk around, peeking out the windows and under the doors, all while I was butt fucking naked. Tony was so damn high that it didn't turn him on anymore. At first, he loved it, but soon, it became part of our little routine. He would puke when we were cooking the rocks, and I would take a hit and get undressed. I would literally hold the trash can, while being naked, as Tony vomited in it and then would stop after the second hit. It was quite the show. After all, I was a freaked-out cokehead in the nude of my own movie, *Hell*.

His uncle would have loved to see that action. If he only knew what was happening in the back unit! His sister was my friend and then my sister got to know her, and we all comingled together in the drug scene. She was a golfer, and the drugs began to affect her game and her life. We later got into some other drugs like meth. What a treat that was. She was also a lesbian, which, in those times, meant it was an underground of people in seedy clubs that had sex with each other and did drugs all day and night.

This went on for a few years. And of course, what happens when you run out of money in between movies and then no pictures come in? The in-fighting happens. We had to go back to his family and then try to do a roommate situation with his friend Dan and cousin Tommy Fatone. Well, we all ended up doing coke together and then it became their life too. It was a cycle of the same shit. Then, Tony fooled around with some girl named Katrina. I heard she was ugly as fuck. But I guess he was tired of the same shit with me and needed a new gig who didn't know he barfed from excitement using coke. I am sure his family was growing tired of our relationship and lives going nowhere. My mom didn't like him. She said he was from a crooked family, and she didn't like that he took me away from her at such a young age. My dad thought he was cool, of course! And my brother and my dad had essentially sold me to Tony Abalone, so they could become Teamsters.

So, Tony and I eventually broke up. I fucked his cousin Tommy to get back at him for having an affair, and then that was that. I remember when we were all living in the Manhattan flat. We were invited to a party in SoHo and decided to turn it down to smoke coke. If we had gone, we would have been the derelicts smoking weed and cigarettes and drinking while a pedophile showed up at the party and took a young girl named Mary. They later found her body in a shallow grave on the shores of a lake near Oneida. She had been sodomized and murdered. The New York Alert Program started because of that incident.

That event had an impact on us. We all couldn't help thinking that we possibly could have saved a life that night if we weren't always so fucked up all the time. That was the start of when the band broke up. The raging with that gang was over, and it was time to move on to other endeavors with other drug addicts.

The last time I saw Tony in person was years later walking on a South Jersey beach. I was in my mid-twenties then. He was drinking and screamed at me to stop. I started to walk over and stepped on a random bee. It stung me and I had to get the stinger out. So, I plopped down on the sand and Tony came over. He squeezed it out and said, "There, it's out. All good."

It was like we were never apart for all those years. It was fucking weird. We said a few words to each other, and I think he knew that I was on meth and a bit distant. I was in my own world. He looked sober, despite the drinking, and just carried on and told me, "Take care! Great seeing you!"

CHAPTER 4: ROLLERCOASTER RIDE OF RELATIONSHIPS—FAR FROM DISNEYLAND

There were tons of other guys after Tony through my late teens. I was probably considered a whore in anyone's opinion, even mine. I dated a pig farmer, an African American Creole, and so on. There was one of every age, religion, color, and race. I did not discriminate. I got into an abusive relationship with the pig farmer. It ended with me running away and him burning all my nice clothes in the yard in a huge bonfire. He had hands the size of a baseball glove that he would use to whack me. I'd go flying across the room at least a couple of feet! Then, I got pregnant again. This time from a married African American guy (such a dumbass as I knew what protection was) and had to have another abortion.

Once, I was invited to a party, where I would meet Frankie, who went by Frankie Ferrari. Why? Because he had two Ferraris, a Harley, and tons of shit. I had thought it was a one-nighter and then it turned into this fast-tracked relationship. I found out his girlfriend left him and took his children to New Jersey. Of course, there was drama between them. We grew to like each other a lot and then I started to experience some emotional moments watching him go into his room and cry about seeing his father shot and killed in front of him (famous story in New York) involving corrupt people in the unions and government. On top of all that, the relationship with his ex-girlfriend was just too much—he was kind of a basket case. He was so good looking and yet was so troubled inside. He had a huge family, and we were in and out of each other's lives for many years as a fling here and there.

The Russian had become a confidante, friend, and father as much as possible by then (even though he knew all along I was not his). Think of a drunk Gene Wilder—that was him 24/7. He signed me out of high school by taking my counselor out to brunch at a famous restaurant and promised I would get my GED. I was sixteen and in 9th grade with all Fs, except for the B in Earth Science and A in World History. Both teachers liked me and were a bit flexible and I used it to my advantage as usual to get by. Although, I did enjoy their classes. He moved me into his place to be his secretary/assistant and then I saw he was back on his taxes from the 1970s and early '80s, and I decided that I didn't want to help clean up that issue. So, I did it for as long as I could.

I used his apartment as home base to keep items and lived all over town, whether it was with Tony or other drug addicts. I would have my on-the-go bag, a drawer, small closet space, a futon sofa, and a recliner that I slept on. I showered, ate, slept for a week after benders, got healthy, and then repeated it all. I'd be gone for a month and then return. Once, he tried to change the locks and I got my cousin's husband to change them back and make me keys. I would spend time there when he was out of town, but then I got ratted out by the neighbors.

Before long, I got shipped off to Vermont. My friend told my dad that she would help get me sober and put me up with some friends. So, she introduced me to her friend who had a house for me to stay at. This is where I met Aaron T, who lived behind a diner in downtown Vermont and who was one of the biggest coke dealers in the state. So, my dad and friend ship me off to this state and it's supposed to be a place for me to get my shit together—for what?

Coke dealer training? As probably expected, I did coke all day, every day, and hung out with tons of guys. I went to the ski resorts and met the inner circle of gangsters of Vermont. Who would have known?

One night, Aaron T wanted to see *Aliens vs. Predator.* He and I had no sexual relationship, but I knew he was crushing. It was pretty obvious. *Plus, why would he just feed me so much coke?* So, we went to the movie, and I told him that I needed a refill on my soda. I left him in there and went to the bar next door and met Davian, another huge coke dealer. He took me back to his place and I left Aaron behind in the movie theater. He had no idea where I was and there were no cell phones, of course.

I got super high and when Davian reached over to kiss me, I overdosed! Yes, right into a full-blown drug-induced seizure. I was foaming at the mouth. He said later that he had to grab a hairbrush and shove it in my mouth to keep me from swallowing my tongue. *Didn't he know he is supposed to turn me to my side? Even I knew that!* I couldn't believe it and couldn't feel places in my mouth that were raw from that stupid Goodie brush for weeks after. I apologized and so did he. He took me back to Aaron T's and said, "Hey, maybe you better not do coke anymore."

I just looked at him like—*You think, asshole? No fucking shit, Captain Obvious! But you go ahead and drive away in your sports car that you got from dealing drugs and ruining people's lives.*

I started to question my Russian dad if this was really all from his genes. He looked at me and said, "Why would you say this? What makes you think this way?"

I said, "No reason. Something feels odd."

He replied, "I always thought you were not from me."

The conversation ended there, but he did say, "No matter what, I will always love you as your dad."

And he did.

CHAPTER 5: JOHN, THE WAITER, AND HIROSHI SAN

I would float around from entourages of drug dealers to guys who I didn't have sex with, but who would feel sorry for me and let me crash so I wasn't completely a homeless person. So, I was never a "dig in the garbage can" type of homeless person. I would maneuver daily to set up time to live with people that would carry me to my next plan. I tried to work and then would get high and not go back. I was the definition of a couch surfer, so I met many people at nightclubs and bars. I would party with them all night, while they bought me drinks and supplied me with coke. Then they would take me back to their hotel room or apartment or we would go eat at a diner. Then I'd usually find out he was a pig married man and I'd go off and usually ring up someone who would let me in, shower, and recuperate, and then I'd repeat it again. So, taking a walk from wherever the fuck I was, was quite normal as I was always walking around pondering life.

I went walking one night and stumbled upon a bar near Madison Square Garden. I looked at the bartender and realized it was Jason, a family friend from my childhood. His sister and her fiancé were with him. We had some drinks and then went to their house and did some coke and weed, and drank until the sun came up. I didn't even have my clothes with me because, at the time, I was living with John, one of my many abusers, who worked at the fanciest restaurant in New York City. So, I borrowed Jason's sister's clothes and went to my friend's house down the street to couch surf there. This was the way of my life. Here, there, and everywhere, the surfer goes.

But that night started me hanging out with this new crew. I stayed with Jason, his sister, Candy, and her boyfriend, Scott, for a while. We tanned in the front yard and then Jason and I got buzzed one night and fucked. It seemed strange, as he was a family friend that I met when I was just eight years old. All I knew was it wasn't right inside—something felt bizarre. I kept hanging out with them and something dawned on me. I asked Candy one day out of the blue, "Hey, did your dad fuck my mom?"

"What? No way! She's Aunty, like our au pair."

After a minute, she said, "I am going to call my dad and find out what he says. I will let you know."

Her dad's name was Javier, and he was a Special Ops Ranger in the Vietnam War and the U.S. Advisor to the South Vietnam General. He retired after years in the service and multiple tours in Nam, but he actually came back to the Bronx quite a bit in the late '60s. In more recent years, he was in Germany with one of his new wives and then moved to Sicily to teach at a college there.

Candy finally reached him over the phone and asked him the question that was starting to bother me more and more. He denied it, of course, and then when she told him that I fucked Jason, he changed his tune. "Okay, it happened only once, I promise."

Then, she asked if I was his daughter, and he said, "Not to my knowledge."

The subject died there as far as Candy was concerned. It was buried. Not for me though.

One day, after Jason borrowed his boss's brand-new scooter, his boss said he had to return it to the bar. Jason had a hatchback that was standard transmission, so I couldn't drive it. I didn't even have my license, let alone know how to drive stick. So, we decided that I would drive the scooter to the bar, and he would follow me in the hatchback. Let's also not forget that we were high all the time. I didn't belong driving any vehicle! I decided that I was going to take a quick detour and drive through Battery Park with the shiny new scooter to show off, even though Jason told me not to take any side streets and to stay on target straight to the bar. I didn't listen, of course. I took a turn into the park and then realized it wasn't right, so I hit the gas and made another sharp left turn only to crash into the Head Chef's car of a nearby restaurant. He was visiting the restaurant and left his children in the vehicle and sadly, they witnessed the next event.

I hit the car full speed ahead, stoned and high as fuck from the blue Peruvian flake with a little Tom Collins to wash it down. As I was about to crash into the car, I saw the older kid's face in the back seat with his mouth open. I could see his teeth and the back of his throat. Then there was a flash where his eyes looked like golf balls on crack. I flew backwards off the scooter into the air about three feet, hit my head on the pavement, and passed out cold.

Numerous witnesses told the story to the police when they arrived. When I came out of it, I saw that my finger was almost cut off from the rearview mirror glass of the scooter. I also had burnt the back of my calf on the muffler, which was what woke me up. I screamed and then dragged myself out from under the scooter that somehow ended up falling on me. I was in excruciating pain. Apparently, I had been dragged by the scooter after doing the air flip, which I guess pulled me under and then slid through and against the gravel on the tarmac-type road. Black tar pebbles were in my legs from my thighs to my calves.

Jason found me and came running over. I told him, "Get out of here! Go and save yourself."

I knew the ambulance, police, and cavalry were on their way. This was not my first incident with the cops coming for me. I didn't have a license and was still underage. I had been a runaway for years. The cops didn't catch me yet and I had been gone since I was fifteen. That was nearly three years ago, as my eighteenth birthday was soon approaching. I was on a forever adventure and became more and more of a derelict as each year passed. Instead of climbing the ladder of success and advancing in school or life towards a career or a J.O.B., I was in the Hoodlum Academy and becoming the best student there.

Jason was talking to someone at the scene who witnessed the entire incident. He was trying to explain that it was just because I didn't know how to drive a scooter. After all, the kids were fine in the car. Couldn't we just let it slide? But the father came out, screaming at me for traumatizing them, making a big scene. When he saw that my thumb was nearly cut off, he walked back to his car and drove away.

I kept telling Jason to leave. We had weed and coke in the car, so it would not work out well for him either with the cops on their way. I knew if I took the fall, he'd be innocently spared. Jason was quiet, meek, and mild. He was not a troublemaker, but I was. It was not fair to subject him to that nonsense. I had scruples and morals even then. So, I again told him to get out of there, and I'd deal with the narcs.

He finally left, begrudgingly, as the scooter was being loaded onto a tow truck and removed from the scene. I had caused a major traffic jam. We pissed several people off on that nice, sunny day. Just then, the ambulance arrived. The cops came over to me, ran my name, and bingo bango fandango, my name came up as a runaway who had been on the run for nearly three years. The police were called several times to places that they thought I was last at, and it became a cat and mouse game. I always outsmarted them and got away. So, this was a miracle to them and not really cool for me. I was the idiot, again.

It was mostly my dad looking for me. He was an enabler, but I loved him to death. He saw the real me and said I was capable of so much more. He agreed that my mother, aka Negative Nancy, drove me to do horrible things. He knew, like I did, that I made the choices, but she drove me out of the house. He also blamed her for his excessive drinking. She would pressure him into a corner, and he would run and drink because he felt horrible about himself. Still, I wasn't ready to see him yet.

The cops put me in handcuffs and smiled as they chained me to the gurney by my wrists and the one ankle that wasn't as fucked up as the other. The officer, with a shit-eating grin, said, "We're taking you to New York Presbyterian Hospital emergency, and then you're done."

Cops back then were as corrupt as can be. They did whatever they wanted to anyone—no matter what. The badge in NYC was a license to fuck you up for no reason and they would get away with it, especially if they knew you were a wise gal or guy. I saw it for myself and many others. And, when you needed real help, it'd be a one-off guy or gal who felt sorry for you at the scene, and the other cops could give two fucks. They beat up or fooled around on their wives and girlfriends. If you were someone who pissed them off once, you were blackballed forever. They probably had a flag and clicked it once, and it was with you forever. They did not like being outfoxed by a young dopehead, much less a female one with a mouth. They would all tell me that.

"Your mouth is going to get you in trouble, Marie."

But at that moment, I was more concerned about if Jason was going to get fired from his job. I always left behind a casualty of some sort, and I did develop a reputation in the community that I was filled with drama and recklessness. That was the last time I saw Jason in person.

The ambulance took me to the hospital. *This wouldn't be my only time in an ambulance. Far from it. It's pretty sad that I knew what the inside of one looked like so well that it could be my bedroom closet. Awful.*

So, the paramedic told me, "You got yourself one day ahead of you."

I said, "I'm fucked, bro."

I arrived at the hospital and got taken in a back door. They expedited the admitting process, and I ended up on another gurney and got chained to that bed. I was told, "If you need to use the restroom, the police must escort you and will wait outside your door and take you back to the bed."

Trust me, they wanted me bad. I hung out with unsavory folks and never got clipped when they arrived. I was always one step ahead. I looked up and there was a nice Swedish doctor who came into the room. He asked me with a big smile, "What do we have here, Miss Marie?"

I turned red and smirked back and said, "Looks like a ton of fucking road rash to me."

He sat down on his rolling stool after scrubbing his hands well. He put on the green nitrile gloves and slowly rolled closer. He looked up at me, close to my face, and asked, "Why is a good-looking girl like you in here and handcuffed to the bed?"

I said, "Right!? Those bastards got the wrong girl!"

He laughed and said to me, "You realize they're going to take you to the naughty girl house down the street?"

"I suppose so."

He took his time and gingerly picked out each rock of asphalt and put it in his stainless bowl. All I could hear was the clink, clink, clink of them dropping in. All the while, he was humming a song. I don't know what it was, but it was so Zen and calming. And I knew he was taking his time to stretch out my length of freedom there. He was cute, tall, and tanned, like he had been enjoying his residency there by going to the Jersey Shore for the weekends! I would take it, especially if it meant a few less hours at the Naughty Girl's Home. Fuck yeah, pick those rocks out one by one honey, then stitch my thumb back on nicely like a plastic surgeon. He did. My thumb was barely attached to my hand and he repaired it. He also made the nasty nurse scrub me instead of him prior to entering the room! She was Nurse Cunty Ratched for sure. Pretty low moment in life and rather embarrassing and painful.

Then, the talk about the third degree burn on my calf. The muffler fried it near to the bone. So, they treated all the areas and it took forever. The cops were fuming. But what could they do? They had to treat me and get me on meds for infection prevention, especially since I was headed to the kiddy jail down the street. I came out of the ER door all patched up, and the cops greeted me and shuffled me into their patrol car, locked the doors, and turned around to tell me, "You're done, girl. We got you now."

I was thinking—*Who gives a fuck, you fat fuck with the badge.*

I arrived at the mini jail that wreaked of Pine-Sol and those damn itchy brown dresses, handmade by someone's aunt, probably. I walked up to the lady at the front desk and saw she was the same one from years past. She told me, "Oh, I see you made it back? Checking in?"

Bitch.

They took me in and the process began. They made me shower with the lice shampoo from head to toe, including my private parts. There was no conditioner for the long hair, of course, and it tangled badly. I then had to put on none other than the brown, itchy polyester dress. PTSD over that thing. It was tight on the top and looked like a potato sack with wrinkles.

When they were done, I sat down while they performed the intake process with the tough chick wearing a badge, giving me the rundown of how I fucked up again. I said, as I always did, "I am not talking to you unless you give me a cigarette and light it for me."

I was tricked once, and they gave me a cigarette and no lighter or match. So, they kept their word and said, "You figure out how to light it."

I learned my lesson. Anyhow, I looked her in the eyes and answered her irritating questions. After a while, I rolled my eyes and cleared my throat, asking for ice water. She told me, "You have no money, no cigarettes, no family to bring it, and bitch, I am not helping you. You can go to lockdown and ponder your own life."

So, I said, "Go ahead!"

She had nowhere to put me because it was clearly overcrowded in there. So, she went to get a cigarette in the front. She came back with Kool Filter Kings—gross ass shit. *Yuck!* I was more of a Benson and Hedges Virginia Slims type of gal. Sleek, sexy, and very *Scarface*—Michelle Pfeiffer style. It was all I had though, so I took a long drag and blew the smoke out slowly right into her face. I giggled disrespectfully—I knew nothing else.

Then I asked, "Can I call my mom for the cigarettes before we go on?"

She said, "Fuck no! Wait until I am done with this process."

I finished her silly interview that was all too familiar, and she called out, "Lombardi wants to use the fucking phone."

Then, to me, she said, "You need your parent's permission to get the person to bring the cigarettes."

So, I called my mom, and she was trying to lecture me. I said, "I am going to hang up and not listen to you if you don't sign the paper for me to smoke cigarettes and receive packs from the outside unrelated people."

She did it, surprisingly. I think she was just relieved that they finally found me, and I was alive. So, I hustled Roberta, my friend that lived down the street from Jason, to bring me a pack and a jacket. She scolded me and said, "Marie, you are always welcome here, but you need to clean up and go back to school."

I said, "Okay," but in my mind, it was—*Nope*.

I was about to turn eighteen in two weeks—I would be an adult and not have to worry about any of this shit. I got a visit from the social worker within 24 hours, during which time I slept on a mattress on the floor. The '80s were a fucking rad time to party and have fun, which often resulted in these facilities being severely overcrowded. I'll leave it there. The social worker told me, "You're eighteen in less than two weeks."

I said, "Yes, I know that."

"There is no room, so we can't keep you in here. It's a waste of space, food, and time."

Waste of food—Wow!

She continued, "You're not ready to change anytime soon and a lost cause."

So, she made a call, and I was fist pumping it past the badge lady who was a cunt and I said, "I am outta here, girls and ladies. See ya bitches on the flip side."

Then I literally skipped to the front doors. They buzzed the door open, handed me my shit I had at the time—mostly the jacket and the pack of Benson and Hedges Menthol Lights long. I waved like Miss America and made the peace sign to the camera at the front of the building. I was off, breathing fresh air and on my next adventure. I was too embarrassed to return to Jason's and I heard Candy and Scott moved back to Upstate New York, near where the gangsters hid in the Adirondacks. She started her own restaurant business there to get away from her demons in the city. Her dad moved down the street from her—a walk or bike distance away.

I was dating Ronnie, a professional skateboard athlete, who played tennis and worked in a high-class restaurant—the type of place where they make Cherries Jubilee and Mango Flambe or Steak Diane with Béarnaise sauce. Yes, he was so proud to be a classy waiter, playing with fire, burning fruit each night, high as a kite around all those wealthy people. Then he would come home with leftover filet mignon with the bearnaise sauce or beef wellington plus escargot and French bread. Dinner was good, but he would beat the fuck out of me, mostly so I would stay home, and he could have me all to himself. I had a black eye every other week. As soon as one would heal, it'd be there again on the other side. I was a prisoner who had to watch his stinky cats.

His apartment could have been nice, but it wasn't. He was a sick fucker. He and his friend Doug, who knew what turmoil I was in, and never helped me. I had met him in a nightclub. Actually, he was sloppy seconds from my sister. She had dated him, but said he was too short for her. He was in great shape, had a cute face, and demonstrated great manners as, after all, he was from the rich side of town in SoHo—where the elite lived. I had moved in with him shortly after starting to date him, which was a tumultuous, on-and-off relationship of hell and desperation. It was just for a regular place to put my head, shower, and what I thought would be to go to the nightclubs when I ran away and the beach during the summer.

The problem was, he didn't let me out of the house. He was so possessive and kept me like a doll in a case. If I went to 7-Eleven to get a Slurpee or a candy bar, he'd slap or choke me. He'd question me like the Spanish Inquisition, and I would pop, as he knew I had a hard time lying. I always told the truth. His apartment was dark and dank. He didn't use his living room, and he had very few belongings. There was a small kitchen, bathroom, bed, TV, and balcony. That was the extent of it. He had a bike and parked it in his litter-box-smelling living room. It was gross. He had some female clothes and a fur coat that belonged to his ex-girlfriend. I thought it was a bit strange that he would have hung on to these items along with some framed pictures of her that he was so careful that I did not fuck with.

The best thing about the apartment was that it was in the prime spot for all the nightclubs. You had Studio 54 on one corner and many others right in the same neighborhood. You could not get into 54 unless you knew the cocaine guy. This was the corner of where hell was located and all the evil vibes that spawned from it. But it was the coolest time to grow up in that scene. It was the best music and people from all over the world! I loved hanging out with the gays—they didn't come on to you and they taught you how to dance and have fun until the sun came up. There were also all the little dive bars in the alleyways with tiny eating spots, so you didn't have to venture into the middle of the city where it was expensive.

The apartment was party central to it all and his balcony had the best view. So, how was a girl in the late '80s, not able to experience this when that was all she knew? He used to tell me that if I left, I would have to tell him my whole day, where I went, who I talked to, everything. And if he found out I lied, he would be pissed and torture me physically and verbally. He lectured me after he slapped or hit me. He didn't stop.

He used to take the telephone with the long cord into the bathroom and stay in there for a while. I mean, one time, it was nearly ninety minutes! I would knock and he would ask me to go away. I felt weird and left out. Maybe he had IBS? I always give others the benefit of the doubt.

One day, I saw him throw his phone bill in the trash. He was angry about it. He crumpled up the paper, grabbed his bike in the living room, and left for his high-end waiter job. I stayed home and discovered that on the bill were all these numbers in Mississippi, Georgia, and other states that were long distance calls out of New York. I didn't fuck him much as I felt—*Why am I going to reward bad behavior if he's knocking me out?* So, I kept that little kitty all to myself and said, "Nope, no one gets it if you fuck with me." So now, here I am looking at this phone bill and was like—*Who the fuck is he calling and staying on the phone with for this long?*

I called one of the numbers and it was a phone sex operator. I was pissed. I couldn't believe this asshole had me, a young, hot chick, and then because I was so bruised up, he had to get it on with old ladies giving him phone sex for all that money he made at the fancy restaurant. He spent all his tips and excess funds on phone sex and that's why he lived simply. When I confronted him on it, I got slapped and beat down to the ground.

I was in this shitty relationship and couldn't help thinking that I thought Tony was bad. He was great compared to this. I was feeling horrible about myself. I looked haggard and was just strung out, trying to understand why he wanted to control and hit me until I'm so ugly? It made no sense.

I got invited to a dinner at the Windows of the World at the top of the World Trade Center. It was the hangout for dinner, drinks, and an elevated crowd. I loved the vibe. It felt so right, and I longed for that as I was living in hell. I knew I had to get out of the ghetto and rut that everyone falls in when they are born and raised in the city with no parents at home. They are meant to stay there, as the cycle just repeats, and each generation does not improve their life.

Reno Fox invited me. He was an actor, entertainer, and brother to professional surfer Rad Fox. He invited me to this gathering of the minds to talk with a potential multimillionaire and Japanese investor. I was to be the "arm candy." Reno was a dear friend. We never dated. He pleaded with the investor that he wanted this opportunity to invest in his tour venture. The sole purpose of my existence that night was to be there to look pretty and help him seal the deal.

I got ready with my makeup and nice outfit and went. It was the one week I did not have a black eye, coincidentally. I had fun. I was finally able to wear nice clothes instead of being in rags. I was out of the prison cell at the apartment while Ronnie was at work making Cherries Jubilee. He had to earn funds so he could afford to pay the phone sex bills.

We were ordering drinks at Windows. There was all this food in front of us and no one was eating. We were all chatting with an amped vibe across the table. The investor was young, and he had this scar in and above his eyebrow—kind of like Jason Momoa, but better. So, I asked him, "Hey, what happened?"

Everyone stopped and stared at me. Then the table got quiet. They looked at me like—*How dare I ask that question*. He looked at me and couldn't speak English. So, he said, "Sumimasen?" (I would find out that means 'pardon me').

I looked around, wondering how this guy was going to know what was happening with this venture when he must have all of it translated, and no one was actively translating. Because I knew he couldn't communicate in English, I started using sign language and playing charades with him at the table. I was able to understand that he was a race car driver (like NASCAR) in Japan, and he got into an accident, which is how he hurt his eye. Then he had plastic surgery to fix it, and it was the best they could do, as the hair did not grow back in the brow area. The Japanese millionaire had his hands under the table so I couldn't see them, but he conveyed that he had to give up that career and instead started an import, export company of luxury cars that were custom-made for the wealthy. Furthermore, he imported leather from Milan, Italy, to be the ultimate soft upholstery in these custom cars.

He had rims that were five thousand dollars each back then for one tire. The car itself was worth hundreds of thousands. *I love me some tires to this day! I am a tire gal.* We were talking in both our native tongues, and we didn't need to know what we were saying. We got it. He was having a blast and couldn't believe we could get along just fine without understanding each other's languages. We totally played charades, and he was crystal clear on what he was talking about. Meanwhile, I'm half Japanese, so Reno looked across the table and had this pissed off look, like I was stealing his thunder. I shrugged and then realized—*Oh no, where is Ronnie?* He would be leaving the restaurant soon and wonder where I was if I didn't beat him home. I was watching the clock constantly and then politely excused myself and told everyone I had to go. Reno was flipping out. I bowed and apologized, then left to go home to Meanie

Weanie Phone Sex Addict Waiter Ronnie. I got in the door and he beat me to it! He did ask where I was, and I had to be honest and tell him. He was pissed off, but no beating that time.

The next day, I received a call, and Reno was telling me that Dwight, Hiroshi's translator, and his manager wanted to meet me at the Four Seasons in the lobby to discuss a potential arrangement. I was beside myself as I didn't know what happened and I wasn't sure what was going on. I was dumbfounded by this invite. I ended up meeting them at the Four Seasons and they proposed that Mr. Hiroshi wanted me to take a trip to Japan, all expenses paid, plus cost of living, including food and payment, to teach Hiroshi English, or some form thereof. I was flabbergasted! I clearly explained I was not the girl for the job, as I had no professional experience with teaching, didn't graduate from high school, and had never been out of the country. I had no passport and I was a wise gal meant to stay in New York City. They kept reassuring me that this would all be handled, and I would have a wonderful time in Tokyo. The end date to return was indefinite. So, now Reno was a bit hurt that his opportunity was blown for the foreign investment, and all they wanted was me to teach this dude English, in another country, all expenses paid. Although it sounded a bit fishy, it was legit—for the most part. We were not arranging any criminal activity. He was offering me a legitimate form of employment and I did not know how to respond as I was a derelict.

I went back to the apartment in hell and told Ronnie of my opportunity and eventually told my dad. But, instead of telling the truth, I made up a story about how this guy was going to help me get into modeling—a dream my 5'3" frame always had. I didn't want them to think this was only an English teacher assignment. They would not have believed it, as I was not capable of being a teacher or anything positive. Not with my track record. They knew I didn't have the credentials, and I knew my dad wouldn't go for it. It had to be something closer to reality then. So, I told my dad of the modeling opportunity to be photographed with his expensive cars. My dad checked out Hiroshi and took me to get my passport and tourist visa from the Japanese Consulate. I obtained everything I needed and then took whatever clothes I had, plus borrowed Ronnie's ex, Abby's, fur coat, and I was off to Chiba, Japan.

I got to the airport with about two grams of coke on me and I was high as a kite. My dad, the photographer, was taking photos of the event, as was his typical behavior. He was so excited that I was going to Japan on my own. I was so young. I went to the bathroom to stash the shit and I don't know what happened, but it sounded like a bunch of cops or guards came in with those black shoes, but that was only my imagination. I always imagined the black shoes under the door. I actually flushed all the coke down the toilet, and was now going to be sober for the first time in a very long time. *Yikes* is all that ran through my mind. I went out, wiped the white off my nose, and went back out and took more fucking pictures for Dad. The only thing I could think about was why did I flush that coke down the toilet? It was good blue Peruvian flake from Colombia.

Hiroshi picked me up at Narita Airport in his Mercedes and apologized for being late as the Ferrari had an issue with a fuel pump. I was now riding in this beautiful car with this nice man, headed toward a toll. He paid some Yen, and we were off to Tokyo Bay International Hotel. It was Tokyo Disneyland and a theater that had ballet and opera events on the same property. So nice and extravagant. There was gold, marble, and brass everywhere. It was shiny and so elevated and on the bay, where you could see fishermen. The water was green and dirty in my opinion. He told me during a lunch on the top floor in the restaurant that this would be my home for the duration of the trip, unless it became longer. This was all with an English translated sentence he had in his pocket. He told me to be ready for dinner later and he would be by in the morning to pick me up. I went to my room and there was a bidet in the toilet, which I had no idea what it was. It took me forever to figure it out. I invited my friend Kriss, the daughter of a cosmetics company, and when she realized I hadn't brought the drugs, she said I was so lucky, as they don't stand for that shit in Japan.

I had massages, real Japanese curry, acupuncture, and people waiting on me. I was being driven everywhere in a nice car, I ate at the finest restaurants, and went sightseeing all over to Ginza, Akasaka, Roppongi, Shibuya, and much more. He learned so much English just from us hanging out there, drinking coffee, tea, eating meals, and sightseeing. By week two, he was already able to put some sentences together in the English language on his own. He smoked weed and was just so happy I was there.

One night, he dropped me off at the lobby and walked me in and then kissed me on the lips. I looked at him and said, "No, this wasn't part of the deal."

I walked off and said, "See you tomorrow."

He never came to my room unless he was with his assistant, Nick, another translator. That was the last time he made a pass at me in Japan. I made it abundantly clear that I was there on a professional basis, not to be his girlfriend.

I started to gain weight while I was there, as I was eating like a pig. He took me out every day and I was living in a hotel. I also had no dope. I called Ronnie a couple of times and he begged me to come back. He told me to ensure I came back with money, so I could pay fucking rent as he spent all his money on weed and phone sex. Then he said he missed me and wanted me to come home.

So, like a total dumbass, I told Hiroshi San some story that I had to pay rent, which was true and that I had to go back to New York. I said I had a sick relative, which was true—my aunt was dying of cancer. She was my mom's older sister, who was my favorite. He actually cried, and I mean sobbed. He was a grown rich man wailing about me leaving him. I think there was another agenda, and maybe Ronnie saved me from another life that would have taken a different turn. To me, that was the silver lining of what Ronnie did for me, even though it was painful. The culture in Japan was amazing. I mean, it was half of my people. It resonated with me in a strange way. It was a remarkable experience for someone my age and where I came from.

Hiroshi handed me a stack of Yen at the airport that equaled $1,500.00, plus what he paid me while I was there. All the while, he was crying and told me he would come to see me or I would come back. I took the money, of course, and went back to dickhead Ronnie. How pathetic was that move? I smoked a ton of Mild 7 cigarettes on the plane and lied to the flight attendant that I was pregnant so I could eat another meal, as I was stressed off of dope for too long. I also knew I was flying straight to be beaten to a pulp and just left a multimillionaire who begged me to stay and live the good life. But I also couldn't help think that he was probably married and had his wife tied up somewhere.

Hiroshi returned to New York multiple times and I accompanied him to the Hamptons to a beautiful mansion with his friends—a young couple from Japan. He would stay at the Four Seasons while in New York. He invited me there, along with a friend, and said we could be served in the suite. I invited my cousin over and we got high in the bathroom, ate his food, drank his alcohol, and then she left. I hung out longer and he went out and got drunk off his ass. He came back and said, "Mariemie," (that's what he called me), "you only want my money and not me or my love." He chuckled and rolled around on the bed.

He said, “Go get money out of my wallet if you need it before you leave. See you later. I don’t want to hang out anymore; it’s one-sided.”

CHAPTER 6: BACK TO DAD'S

After one last time of Ronnie slamming my hand in his apartment front door, breaking three of my fingers in the process, I woke the fuck up. I left him, went to the hospital, and had three thick silver splints put on my hand.

The nurse shook her head and said, "You need to leave this guy before he kills you."

My friend Jack picked me up and lectured me. I promised him that I would finally leave. And I did.

I moved back into my dad's apartment, which really had no room for two people on a full-time basis. My dad was in denial about me and was happy to have a relationship with me even though it was not your typical or average one. My dad and mom didn't speak much as they were newly divorced in that decade and still hadn't made peace. I only saw my mom here and there since I ran away at fifteen. I'd stop by and pick up necessities like toothpaste and shampoo. That was her way of contributing—toothpaste, and telling me that I was a fuckup and needed to get a job and change my life.

It was a one-bedroom, one-bathroom apartment in the heart of the East Bronx where Dad also worked from. He offered to fix it up and add a futon, so I would have a place to crash and share the kitchen and bathroom. Sounded good to me—it was a roof over my head in town, for free, without some asshole choking me to death. This was the same setup we did when he signed me out of high school with the counselor by taking him to brunch at a local spot. Dad did so many deals there and had wonderful luck. It was the best place for Eggs Benedict. So, here I was again trying to get my shit together, living in Dad's office/apartment and eating Eggs Bennie at these client brunches as his sidekick, deadbeat daughter who lost her way AGAIN.

I met up with an old friend, Denny, and we started hanging out again. He and I did a shit ton of coke with my brother and my other sister-in-law back in '86-'87. We used to stay up for nights on end and play Trumps. He was Japanese and knew my siblings from high school. He was ten years my senior and we got along like brother and sister from another mister. He made the best mixed tapes and introduced me to INXS—one of my favorite bands. Denny picked me up one night from Dad's to go to a house in the Village that had the "good shit." I threw on a shirt of my dad's and we went out to play some cards at this guy Daniel's place. I was playing cards, and this couple walked in. Behind them was this tall, handsome dude with a laundry basket in his hand. I turned around and said, "Hi, I'm Marie."

His name was Pauly. He dropped the laundry basket and stumbled up the stairs. He was about 6'1", with dark features, and seemed to be Portuguese, Spanish, and Italian. He had some sexy black gym shorts on with hairy legs. He joined us at the game in the living room with this large smile and then invited Denny, Daniel, and me to partake in some high-quality blow. We obliged, obviously.

That night was the beginning of a relationship that lasted several months. We started to get a little serious and would both sleep over at each other's places as Dad was always working on set, so the place was all mine to entertain. We fucked in Dad's bed a lot. (Sorry, Dad.) He sang Rose Royce songs to me, and I about died as I really thought we were in love, and it was real. But unfortunately, he was truly in love with his girlfriend that left him. She was his first love from their high school days, which was a bond that I couldn't top. I was the rebound clown. Yup, the one that was keeping him company while he mourned the loss of her.

We went back and forth, and then I had had it. I couldn't be second choice anymore. One day, Daniel, who was dating my cousin, asked me to go with him to unplug from both our relationships. We commiserated and hung out in Vermont, then jumped on a plane to stay with my sister. Pauly called one day and begged me to come back, so we could give it another try. I felt like he was forcing me to fill the void. I believe he loved me in some way, but he longed for Jody. Still, I went back to him.

We had great sex, laughs, and he treated me well by taking me to dinners, introducing me to his friends, and living the more elevated way of life that I loved. This went on and off for a couple months. One night, he came to take me to a movie, but I had fallen asleep on my dad's lazy boy. I wasn't doing much sleeping during that time as I was hitting the meth hard and was usually up for days at a time. The coke wasn't doing it for me anymore. Plus, it made me paranoid. It also became very expensive, and I was tired of getting it by being someone's arm candy or girlfriend. I wanted my own shit. My dad knew something was going on, so he told Pauly that I was sleeping and that was the end of that. He never returned or called until we hooked up one last time. I had sex with him and then that was it. We never saw each other again. It was sad. I had asked him earlier if he ever wanted kids, and he said he wasn't ready for it. Maybe I knew I was going to become pregnant.

I went on months of escapades of hanging with a huge meth dealer, who was married and wanted me as well. It was a very peculiar relationship. He was obsessed and would wait in his car for hours until I got home or woke up. My dad thought he was a lunatic, and he was right. I went on to hang with other shady dealers during this time. Life became scary and I was in deep with the squalid. I had no idea I was pregnant with Pauly's child. I also caught Chlamydia from this freak guy in the city and didn't know I had it. It was my first STD.

I went to a house one night and met this man named Rathe. Tall, dark, handsome, and Italian. He was tied to the Mafia, as he was born into it. He was visiting a friend, another druggie in the hood, who was from Jersey. We hung out and he was nice but was a shooter—with a needle—and he used to speedball and then getting really wigged out after he did a hit or a slam. But there was something about him that I was attracted to and he liked me as well. He was fourteen years my senior. Nothing new, right? Older men, drugs, and a wicked situation. *Just the guy I wanted to end up with.* He became the new toy. He came into an insurance settlement of thousands of dollars and asked if I wanted to visit Jersey in the country and see if I liked it there. Off I went on another adventure. I loved Jersey. My sister had moved there with her kids and I visited often, so I was familiar with the lay of the land. But not where he was about to take me...

CHAPTER 7: THE GANGSTER AND MY LOVE FOR JERSEY

I traveled to Jersey and Rathe picked me up. I was exhausted and fell asleep in the brown standard Honda Civic. So unassuming for a gangster. He lived in a village-type situation—a sacred place not easy to get to. The road was dangerous and more than twelve miles in from the area where it got tricky. There were cliffs with hundreds of feet below and no guardrails with dirt and gravel roads. I woke up and immediately looked around. It was pitch black. I looked to my right and saw an image of an animal. It was white, with shadows, and it had red eyes! It was massive, galloped like a horse, and stared at us through the windshield. It crossed the road in front of Rathe's little car. I screamed at Rathe, "What the fuck was that?"

He said, "You don't mess with the White Stag. He guards Oswego Lake and other legends are in this area. It's sacred."

I wanted to scream and freaked out that he was taking me to a scary place in the middle of nowhere. Yet, I somehow knew that if you don't respect them from this realm, it is a negative frequency you are putting out into the Universe. And I certainly did not want to be its enemy. He said that he picked up Jenny Jump, a survivor, who looked like an angel one night on the side of the road, and she disappeared from the back seat of his car. His dad, a near pure Italian man told him that you always help them if they ask, and you will never be punished. They will leave you alone. The Jersey Devil is another creature in the Pinelands.

Rathe and I moved in together in a house that we couldn't afford, located in an upscale neighborhood in Jersey, known as the Alpine. I started to feel awkward and gain weight around my midsection. My boobs got huge. We went to the doctor, and she said, "You are six months pregnant!"

"Holy shit!" was all I could manage.

She walked out of the room and Rathe looked at me dead center and asked, "It's not mine, is it?"

"I guess not," I said, as the math didn't add up.

He said, "Well, I love you and it doesn't matter. We don't say anything to your family or mine and will just raise him as if he were mine."

I thought that was fucking cool as fuck. I mean, he didn't have to do that, and he must have loved me to take on that burden at such an early phase of our relationship. The doctor took a test and told us that I also had Chlamydia. I knew it was from a low-life drug dealer I had had a fling with. She put me on Erythromycin and gave a prescription to Rathe as a precaution. I got super sick and Rathe had to rush me to the hospital. I recovered, but that was a horrible ride down the longest highway of my life, it seemed. We lived on our own until we ran out of money from his settlement. He was a liar and would go and visit his other son and say he was going to work. We had no choice but to move back to the sacred village in Jersey with his parents. This time, for a while.

I finished off my pregnancy and I didn't get high. I was sober and I felt great. I had a baby coming and we were fixing up the place from a single wall construction plywood structure to having drywall and separate bedrooms. It was cute and we were with his parents, so I'd have company while he went on his monthly benders. I gave birth to Ace, Rathe's son, in June of 1990, after two days of complications. He was super white just like his biological father, Pauly, and looked like the both of us, and definitely not Rathe. Rathe told his parents that he pulled more on my side. That was a loving act to take the hit and know that his parents knew the truth. Especially his father, Pops.

Rathe was well connected with the Mafia. His mother, Lulu, was the sister of a head Mafia guy. Rathe had protection from Uncle Tommy Barone and many other dangerous people. I was sheltered from knowing anything in particular, but the vibes just weren't right.

Rathe went out one night in his car and came back shook up and distant. I later found out that he was involved in a shooting. We married during this period, and then had to go to court after he was arrested for the shooting. I thought his future looked grim, but he had a terrific lawyer that proved otherwise. We beat the case and went on with our lives. I knew Rathe was a terrifying person. I could feel it. He left me home in that village often with no running water and no resources. I had to have a cousin get buckets of water from the nearby river, so I could bathe my baby. Rathe was a huge coke and heroin addict, and of course, spent any money that he had, charged up the credit card, and was up to no good with his friends. He would come into a lot of money, and it would be gone quickly. Then he would go to a place where he lived with his parents that had water from the mountain tap (like a pipe into the mountain)—free food, rent, fish. He used it as his dry out place. This is where we lived for a number of years.

We managed to finagle a Section 8 housing assistance program option and moved out of the village and back to Alpine. It was truly a beautiful place. It had a lot of trees and greenery, and that's what made it so unique. Plus, it seemed like a world away from the dark and dingy city. It just resonated with my soul. I was used to the fire trucks, sirens, and people screaming all the time.

During this point of the marriage and life with our new son, drugs reentered the picture. Of course, Rathe and I both got into coke again and then the meth was making a comeback from the crank days. They had perfected the formula, and you could lose tons of weight rapidly, all while feeling like Superman or Superwoman. The shit kept you up for days and weeks. You would have the cleanest and most organized house. People went absolutely and literally insane. It was probably the worst meth epidemic in the U.S. for a number of years. While my in-laws would watch Ace, Rathe and I flew to Upstate New York to do side deals we had no business partaking in. Eventually, we moved up there. One day, he left me at a drug dealer's house and went off to use all the product and money from the investors. I was in a bad spot. During this same trip, a man named Jesse came to the house to trade a gold chain for dope from us. Rathe called me in from the back bedroom to analyze the jewelry and to be the second one to judge the guy.

Jesse started hounding me after that day we met. He wouldn't leave me alone, and he finally broke me down. We started to canoodle, for lack of a better way of putting it. My relationship with Rathe was on its way south, as he was awful toward the end of our relationship. It was toxic. We had a cousin from my side living with us, and she was renting the room, cooking, and helping me take care of my son, Ace. We all started to use meth and it just ripped through our family. We were lucky we had a roof over our heads.

Rathe went to Block Island to work for one week as we needed money to live and buy more coke and meth. And while he was gone, Jesse contacted me and came over. My cousin warned me that I was playing with fire and that it wasn't right—she didn't care for Jesse. She was right, of course. *So, did I listen? No.*

She left to head back to the city and saw Rathe at the airport in passing. She told him there were issues back at the house and that this guy, Jesse, had been coming around. He called me up and Jesse was right there. Thinking he was still in Block Island, I played the role of being alone with my son in our home. At that time, there was an airline that traveled from the city to the Upstate New York airport and there were midnight flights. Hardly anyone caught them, but that night, guess who did? Rathe. He had a taxi drop him off at the top of the lane. We lived in the last house at the bottom toward the horse pasture in the motherfucking boonies. So, he walked around the house with his gray badass cowboy boots and Jesse said he could sense someone outside.

"No one is out there!" I said calmly.

Well, he sure was. He looked and listened by the bedroom. He heard us talking, and when I went into the bathroom, he spoke to me through the high bathroom window in a whisper, saying that we were busted. I screamed like it was the boogeyman outside. He then came to the solid kitchen door and kicked it right open with his boot. There were only two doors in and out of that house and Jesse fled as fast as he could out the front door and left me behind. I had no underwear on and only a striped green and blue Ralph Lauren T-shirt that didn't cover my ass. He grabbed me and pinned me up by my neck and held me up in my cousin's room against her door. He stuck his hand right into my vagina, smelled it, and went nuts. That was the longest terrorizing abuse up to that point that I had ever experienced. He was furious.

"You are my wife, and you fucked that loser? How could you?"

He just blew up and kept hitting and torturing me. I understood that what I did was wrong, but Rathe put me through some really difficult times throughout our marriage. He would disappear for days or weeks at a time and spend all our money, leaving me and our son with nothing. I felt it was my passive-aggressive way of getting back at him. Yes, I should have broken it off, and then went on with my business. But I didn't.

He ripped out all the phone cords from the wall and I was held captive for hours. Until finally, hours later, I managed to beg that I wanted to call my dad and just talk. I even tried to call Hiroshi San. I had his number memorized. But I couldn't get through as the time difference was half a day ahead of New York. So, he gave in and said that I could call my dad. I dialed my sister Kate, who lived up the street. She could tell by the tone of my voice that I was in danger. She talked me through it.

She said, "Don't answer anything else, just say yes or no. Do you need the cops?"

"Yes."

"Should I come over with the cops?"

"Yes."

The cops came and arrested him, and my sister and her two sons came over. Poor kids, they witnessed so much shit from me. The police later released Rathe, and he was still on the warpath. I threw all his clothes in bags on the front lawn and asked him to remove them. He broke in the house when I wasn't home and slashed all my nice dresses with a big X in the back and hung them back up in their place.

During all this, Jesse was at a hotel, showering, chilling, and getting high. While I was dealing with all this shit. He never even came back to see if I was okay. I got in touch with him and couldn't understand why he was such a pansy and left me. He had no balls to stand up. Rathe had even said that—he was a coward for not helping me and getting his ass kicked like a real man if he wanted to fuck someone else's wife. I couldn't blame Rathe there. He was right and

I knew it in my heart too. It was over, and Rathe went his separate way. The next day, I allowed Jesse to meet me at my sister's, where I was hiding out.

Wise
Marie
by Natasha Brune
VOLUME 1

CHAPTER 8: THE DEVIL INCARNATE AND FATHER OF THE KORN

Jesse and I then became a couple. He lived with me in my house for a while, but it wasn't his scene in the country. Mostly, there was no dope close by or even in town or the next one over. Upstate New York was still pretty innocent then, and spared from the meth epidemic. He took me back to the city, as that was the goldmine for meth production—it was everywhere. He convinced me to move out of that house where I only paid ninety-two dollars a month in rent due to the assistance I was receiving. Not a well thought out move, but I did not belong on government assistance. I was the perfect example of being capable to earn my own living. But I was stubborn as fuck and in denial.

So, I uprooted my son, Ace, and we moved out of the house that I was nearly beaten to death in. We shipped the furniture to the city and placed it in storage until we knew where we were going. All my life's belongings were in there, including photos, jewelry, clothes, furniture, and other valuable and irreplaceable items. I now had a son and no home. Jesse moved us to one of his many long- or short-term hotels, with me living out of a backpack with a baby. I actually moved back to Dad's at one point, and we would sleep there and then go with Jesse when he would sneak us out. My dad was worried sick, but once again, he was busy with the films in the city. I used my dad's car and dragged my son from house to house, hotel to Dad's, and so on. He never used his car in the city anyway.

It was during this time that I began to notice unexplainable bruises on Ace's arms and body. And it was clear he was petrified of Jesse. I could tell something wasn't right. He used to cry and be out of breath. It was painful. My gut told me something was seriously wrong. Jesse had a daughter from a previous serious relationship, but they had never married. That little girl was about eight at the time. She was spoiled by him, and she could do no wrong in his eyes, so of course that made Ace and me feel like shit. We had to have her with us at times and the mix wasn't comfortable. He was mean to my son and to me in front of her. When I would question Jesse about Ace, he would snap, and later, I found out he took it out on Ace. When he would talk to Ace, Ace would start hyperventilating and not being able to breathe or complete his sentence. Over time, he started to stutter. That's when I knew there was abuse happening, but I couldn't prove it. Jesse had also started in on me and I noticed he liked to hit me in the head, because no one would see it there as I have thick, long, and wavy hair that easily covered all the bruises. He was experienced at this. Not his first rodeo, for sure.

I became fed up after an incident at the Lufthansa Cargo parking lot. I was using my dad's Buick (he downsized and finally got rid of his Cadillac habit) to run errands for him, and I had to ship an item to Rhode Island. I left Ace in his car seat with Jesse per his instructions, so I could be faster in line at the counter. Ace started hyperventilating, and I told Jesse that I could take him with me. He yelled at me to hurry the fuck up and just get the task done at cargo. So, I listened. But he soon came into the facility and pulled me out, hurrying me out of that place. He said to get the fuck in the car and that we had to leave quickly. Ace was screaming, and I had no idea what was going on. I asked what happened and of course was told to shut the fuck up. I believe I got slapped and both Ace and I were crying, and my head was spinning. I didn't know what I did wrong.

I was screaming in the car and Ace was shaking and hyperventilating.

Some time passed and my dad returned home. He was working on a movie and had met up with a former friend, falling in love after all these years of being hurt from my mom. He was preparing to move to a farm in the county with tons of fruit and walnut trees. Sue Anne had a long lease there with a huge farm and a guesthouse on it. She had helpers that worked the farm and tons of space for Dad's equipment and belongings. He called me and asked me to come to the apartment, but not to come upstairs, while he was in the city after being done with a film. He asked me to wait in the back parking lot by the school and to just watch from the street into his office window that was visible from the road. I watched and saw a police officer talking with my dad at his desk. My dad was taking notes and appearing to be looking at his desk calendar. The cop left and my dad signaled me to come up. He sat me down at his desk and said, "We have a problem with that guy Jesse you are seeing."

"Like what?"

I was thinking he was in trouble with the law as that wasn't all that far-fetched. He began to describe the Lufthansa Air Cargo parking incident, and right away, my heart sunk, and I knew that it was the day I couldn't figure out what we did wrong at the airport.

Apparently, a woman pulled up next to Jesse in my dad's car. She witnessed the horrific scene of physical and verbal abuse against my son, which turned into horror. She took down the license plate number and started to tell Jesse off and threatened to call the police, which she did, and that's how they found my dad to relay the story. The cop said that guy was sick and mean to the young boy and advised him to have me file a TRO. *Did I listen? Nope.* Stupid, battered wife syndrome, selfish and hurtful. I can't explain it to where a normal non-abused person would understand. But anyone who has been abused knows, it feels like a combination of hurt, fear, love, disbelief, and hope. Sick, I know. We humans and our paradigms.

I was furious and hurt. I told Jesse we were done and to leave me the fuck alone. I left town and went to the country again. I was trying to be strong to protect my child and myself. That area was my sanctuary through tough times in my life, and I was familiar in those surroundings. I brought Ace with me, and we moved to my brother's house in Buffalo. We brought our stuff from storage and then lived there for a bit. I got tired of it as I really didn't get along with my brother and decided to stay at our friend Kyle's house down the street from there. He was an orchid farmer and knew my brothers for years. He wanted to help me out, so he allowed me to stay in one of his rooms. Ky kept it a secret, but somehow Jesse found out—he always did. There was a guy named Eddie that came over one night to hang with Ky and, of course, do drugs. That was another reason I wanted to live there. It was my kind of drugs. My brother was still into coke. I had moved on to the next level of meth.

Jesse snuck into Ky's yard in the depths of the Adirondacks in the pitch black. He tried to come to the door and Ky told him to go away and that we were not to be bothered. Ky told me to hide Ace, and I went into a room, afraid for our lives. I had imagined being dragged out of there and then tortured or perhaps killed for running away. This guy Eddie saw how scared we were and was like, "Come out from hiding and relax. This guy isn't going to hurt you."

I said, "Oh, yes he is."

Eddie said, "Watch this."

He yelled, "Get the fuck out of here, you punk."

He shot his gun once or twice and Jesse was gone in a heartbeat, that pansy. Eddie looked at me and said, "I told you."

He grabbed my son and put him on his lap and said, "Braddah, don't worry, Uncle got rid of the bad guy. You're safe, boy."

My son, only two at the time, fell in love with Eddie. So did I, in a way, as a dark angel in disguise from somewhere.

My son and I were embarrassed. Eddie came over every day after that to check on us and then we moved in with Eddie, as he promised to take care of us and never let anyone hurt my boy. I truly believed him. We were safe for a couple months in a nice, elevated townhouse up the street from Ky's. I got to know Eddie's family well and we had our place downstairs in his dad's three-story townhouse. Eddie's brother, Dave, was also a badass, and most feared him as well. Nice looking, smart, upper-class Italians, but still scary, which we loved, as they were on our side. The dad's name was "Cowboy," an old gangster that I didn't realize was someone you didn't fuck with. Eddie told Cowboy and his wife, Martha, plus the kids, that we were there indefinitely to protect us from Jesse. Cowboy said, "No motherfucker is going to hurt this girl and her kid."

So, they became our security guards, and we were loaned a white Buick car with AC, tinted windows, money from Eddie, and a nice place to call home. My son was finally stoked and acting like a regular kid—well, kind of. He was happy, had toys to play with, and loved being in his nice home with other kids. Most importantly, he and I were safe.

I reached out to some old girlfriends from the past and told them about Eddie. They all wanted to meet him, so I invited them to hang out. One of them impressed Eddie, as she was beautiful. I had really thought she was my good friend, but later found her number written on a piece of paper that Eddie had dropped in the living room. I was puzzled and thought it was probably a mistake. Maybe she just wanted to score meth from him directly, or something reasonable like that. I trusted Eddie and her. *I mean, why not, right?* Well, he ended up falling in love with her, and he was a charmer, so I can see why and how. It was a bummer, but it wasn't meant to be that we stayed together. It wasn't destiny. I begged him to stay with me as I didn't want to return to Jesse, but once he found out I was pregnant with Jesse's child, it only sealed the deal, with him moving in a direction far away from me.

And so it was that Eddie and that friend became a couple, just at the same time that I found out I was four months pregnant with Jesse's baby girl. The only downfall in me going back (yes, I realize there were a million downfalls) was that my dad had moved out of that apartment and only had a month or so left on the lease. It was an empty apartment with no furniture or love or Dad. I was going to have to move with him to the country, which was not a possibility, as he was marrying a tried-and-true Jehovah's Witness, Sue Anne. I was an unwed mother, with child two on the way, and full of baggage, both figurative and literal.

Sue Anne did not like me. After all, I was the ultimate sinner in her eyes and an embarrassment to her and her Kingdom Hall friends. I had no choice but to become homeless or go back to Jesse. I tried to do it on my own and I did not make it. And he came swooping in and promised he would never hit Ace or me again and that this new baby was everything to him and he would do anything for us all. Boy, was that a line of shit. I was vulnerable and homeless. He said that he would do his best to support us, and we started residing in hotels again. We'd pack up and unpack, then do it all over again day after day, week after week. The hotels knew who we were, and we fought all the time and in public. I had to catch the bus to the emergency room with a two-year-old who was traumatized with major PTSD. Pathetic.

A friend suggested that I start working at a sleezy club on the lower part of town, as the construction workers and union guys would drink before going home to their wives. Jesse flipped out and paced back and forth while I reported to work. I knew he was outside the bar, so I couldn't relax and allow myself to get trained. I met a girl named Kathy there, who became an ally and friend. She was good to me. I couldn't continue though, as it wasn't my thing to drink with strangers or repeat customers and let them come on to me for tips. I spent more time in the kitchen talking to the Mama San cook and learning how to make kimchi and the best steak ever.

In the meantime, Jesse was desperate and offered to steal the world, so I didn't have to work there. So, I entrusted him once again and decided to let him support us. He moved us into a place with no kitchen and two double beds. He beat the shit out of us at this old hotel near a lake. I can't even remember what the name was. I only remember the water and a restaurant. What a horrible memory. It was a motel building with a front and back entrance, no security, and one person at the front desk. He cased it out and it had the perfect setup for a criminal: side stair exits on both sides of the building, and a parking lot that was open to the public with no gates or obstructions (and that meant two ways to get out). It also had a restaurant downstairs that he loved as they catered to him, and he tipped the old Japanese lady well. She loved him as she didn't know he was the fucking devil incarnate. The demographic that frequented this place was as follows: fishermen, guys that fooled around on their wives with the whores around the corner, prostitutes, and us drug addicts. The hotel unit had no kitchen, but of course Jesse had to sidestep that and get a larger cooler with ice and then a hot plate and started cooking steaks and shit in the room, which caused tons of smoke and the fire alarms to go off. He was such a problematic rule breaker and always testing the system. The inn kicked us out and called the cops.

Soon thereafter, I went into labor with our baby at the Queen's Hospital, not far from there. It was a less crowded situation, and the birth was going well until she didn't come out right away. She was my smallest baby, weighing 5 pounds, 8 ounces, but a long baby at 22 inches. She was born after midnight on Mother's Day 1992. As soon as she came out, he was her knight in shining armor. You could not get in the way of those two. He knew she was his, as she looked just like him, especially the nose! He was smitten, as she had dark hair and different features from his other daughter, who pulled a blonde look. He would constantly say things like, "This baby is best and just like her dad." He carried her and marveled at how she was the best daughter ever.

As a baby, Leah didn't cry or whine. She just screamed for food, a necessity, as he would say over and over. Ace was dog shit, and he loved on her constantly. Ace would look at me like he was made of a disease, as he was abused all the time now. Leah was one of the best babies ever in terms of not driving me nuts crying. I believe at the time, God knew I had enough that was happening, and so he blessed me with a cool baby, but the devil incarnate got into her spirit eventually. She had a mellow vibe and didn't wig out like most babies do. She drank her powdered SMA milk, as I didn't nurse her for obvious reasons. She just needed a dry diaper and air conditioning, so she didn't sweat profusely like her father. And she would sleep for hours and leave us alone. Everyone wanted to babysit her, which was a savior for Ace and me. I named her after my brother Peter's girlfriend (ex at the time), and she was actually a very good friend of mine.

All the praise on Leah made Ace feel even more insecure and like he could never live up to the new baby. He was an outsider, and of course, poorly treated. He started to get the same way again around Jesse, and I knew the abuse must have started when Jesse would insist on taking him on errands with him minus Leah and me.

There were secret beatings, and then Ace would be quiet for hours in a corner. When you would ask him a question, like, "Are you hungry?" he would start hyperventilating and do the huffing and stuttering thing.

I kept telling Jesse, "You can't take him alone anywhere."

Then I would get my ass kicked for accusing him of abuse. We got kicked out of that inn on the night we went to the Reggae Splash Concert. He loved that kind of music. "Black Roses" was one of his favorite songs.

We went to the front desk to discover that they had seized our belongings and locked us out of the hotel room. We had to leave Leah with Jesse's mother for the night to figure out what we were going to do and where the next place was that we would call home. Traveling drug addicts do not typically have much of a home. This was when he had us showering at the Bellevue Hospital in the employee's locker rooms on the ground floor. I had to do it or I would get beat, yelled at, or he wouldn't take me anywhere that I could shower at. We were homeless couch surfers, but at least we were clean. I took great care of my kids. It was back to the same routine. He would dump us at a hotel, leave for the hustle, be gone all night, and then return while I was checking out with a toddler and a newborn baby. Pack and unpack. I still have the tick when I unpack and pack. It brings on unbeknownst PTSD in me, and others notice it when they are in a hotel room with me.

Jesse would either move us to another hotel, stay at the current one and pay another night, take us on the road to the next series of events, or linger at a friend's house where the friend sold drugs, all with two children. *How uncomfortable was that?* He would fuck other women and steal anything to get dope, and then cash out to feed and house us (after he got his dope, of course). Sometimes, we would be in a living room for hours, while he was in a bedroom with a woman, and I sat there like I had nothing better to do while he got a blow job or two. *I was definitely not in my right mind!* It was so embarrassing as a mother and partner to him. I couldn't leave or defend myself, as it was back to the normal forms of abuse, and it was getting worse by the week.

I met another abuse victim, the wife of a drug dealer. She and I would compare bruises—we were kindred spirits with PTSD. We would get high and laugh. She gave me pretty dresses that girls would trade her for dope, and she would say, "You're the only one who would look nice in this. Save it for the right moment, girl."

And I always did. They were black, with pearl buttons and rhinestones, velvet cocktail dresses, and A-line skirts.

I finally gave Jesse an ultimatum and said we needed a permanent place to stay, and if he couldn't provide it, I was going to look at options and possibly go back to the country where I could raise my kids with no temptation and not be in the city streets with two kids. He wasn't going to allow that. So, he managed to rip someone off and we magically had the deposit and first month's rent in a couple weeks. We moved into an apartment where it became a living hell. It was a roomy one-bedroom unit with two doors, an entrance at the front with a screen door and a back door from the bedroom that was terrific for him to sneak out from the police or me. It had two-sided parking and tons of ways to escape if he was running. A special task force team was looking for him, so these were his priorities. He was what you would refer to as a thief in the night, literally. He was in heaven with the location, as it was out of the city, but close enough for all the drugs and items to steal to feed his drug habit and give us the gravy to live off of.

The galley-style kitchen and coin washer dryer situation down the dark walkway was a treat. There was a shower stall and a closet, which to us, was nice, as we didn't have to sleep in the car, at a friend's, or in a strange hotel for a change. We installed a portable air conditioner and made it look sweet with new carpet. I moved my furniture in from storage, added a playpen, a stereo with speakers, a DVD player, and a TV, and we were set. We had a large and heavy stolen piece of granite placed on bricks that we used as our eating table. He had some bed frame he ripped off and we put our mattress on it, which worked out fine. The dresser, a crib, and all our belongings fit nicely. Perfect for our little family. Ace was miserable and was so confused on where home was. All he wanted was to go back to Rathe—the only father he knew. He hated the city, the apartment, and that we were trapped all the time with Jesse.

We had family that would come over and help to babysit and then hang out. It was a cool place to live until he became extremely violent and then the neighbors called the police over and over. There we were again, being a disturbance to the peace and hood. How neighborly of us. So embarrassing! Eventually, I had to kick him out or I would be evicted with the kids. The landlord lived on-site and worked at the owner's lodge in the country. She would ask me often, "Why would you stay with a creep like that who beats your boy and you?"

She said, "You're not that dumb."

He was stealing from all these stores and places to pay bills and supply his enormous meth habit, which was growing heavier by the week. I did meth too, but there was never enough to share with me, so I guess it helped to keep my consumption lower—and rightfully so, as I had two children to take care of, and it probably added years to my life. He would leave for long periods of time, and I knew he was being unfaithful. Then he'd beat on me and tell me I was the cunt over and over. That goes right into your subconscious, and you begin to believe it to be true. You don't hear anything positive and that is all you have, day in and day out. Abuse—physical, verbal, and mental. You are made to feel lost and pathetic. I am surprised I didn't step in front of a bus. What kept me alive? My kids.

There was a time when he picked me up, took me to his ex-girlfriend's house that he had the kid with, and left me in the car while he went there to pick something up, apparently. I asked where his hat went, and he said that he left it upstairs and he'd get it back when he saw his daughter next. His ex called me one day and told me he left his hat there, and I said I knew, and she could put it in the daughter's bag when she was to stay with us next. She told me that he left his hat there as they had sex while I was waiting in the car downstairs. She knew I was there, and she fucked him anyway. Sick bitch. And that wasn't his car. It was my sister-in-law, Tiare's car. Who the fuck does that? The devil incarnate, of course.

She gloated about continuing to fuck him and that he was so madly obsessed with her. She was cruel to the core in the most passive-aggressive way. She sent her daughter to private school, and he had to help pay for that too. Boy, was the pressure on. It's even sadder that he was a painter and carpenter by trade and had the opportunity and potential to make a lot of money if he chose. Well, he did choose. He chose meth and a life of crime and abuse.

Jesse was living from hotel to hotel and would come and terrorize me at the apartment until I finally put my foot down by changing the locks, putting in extra precautions, and filing a TRO. It was getting ridiculous. My sister was visiting one day from upstate with her boyfriend, who was a ranger with the forestry division. Her kids, my nephews, were there. I went into the bedroom as I heard something and then discovered that Jesse was in our bathroom, taking a shower. I looked at him and asked him what he was doing. I told him he couldn't be there. But he just continued to shower and told me to fuck off. He broke in through the back door! Then he got dressed, locked the bedroom door that led to the living room where I had my guests, aka family and the forestry guy.

He put me in a choke hold and then punched me so hard in the face and left eye. I was knocked over and felt myself in a seizure or something that made me rattle, literally. The blood vessels broke in both eyes, so I had no white around my brown eyes, only red. I resembled the lady from the movie *The Grudge!* There was a huge lump the size of a small potato on my upper left forehead. I had two black eyes, and he went out of the bedroom, grabbed ice from the freezer, shoved it in a sock, and walked back in the room. I was shaking on the ground, and I couldn't move.

My sister was in shock. She had no idea he was even there and knew he was supposed to be 100 feet away from us due to the TRO. He proceeded to press the lump on my forehead down with the sock. It was so sore. He was now panicking and shaking me to wake me up. I was nearly knocked out, and Kate threatened to break down the door and call the police. I could hear her, as if she was down a long hallway with an echo. I remember the chilling screams from her two kids and the stuttering from Ace. When she opened the door and saw me on the ground, she kicked him in the nuts and stomach full tilt and MMA pushed him with her leg out the back door and then threw his shoes after him. The neighbors were watching from the windows like it was the best show they'd seen in a while. She called 911, and her boyfriend was wigging out and asking me, "What do you see in him? He's ugly, sis."

Bro! My head is spinning out and I feel lightheaded and in so much pain, I am turning numb. I don't need to be lectured and told I am prettier and deserve better. I am so tired of hearing the "Potential Speech."

Poor Ace was hiding behind the couch and probably peed in his pants again and puked, I'd imagine. He would vomit from the stress.

My nephews protected him and pulled him to play to avoid seeing that I was severely injured. He was crying, "Mommy, Mommy, I want Mommy. Where is Mommy?" They met us at the Bellevue Hospital where I was treated for the injuries. A social worker came in and asked my sister to take Ace with her to save his life. She could not. She worked full-time for the airlines and had her own kids. She was in a similar situation a year prior, and that monster was still in jail for life. He nearly killed her as well. I begged my sister to take Ace with her back to the country. She told me it wasn't happening because she worked six to seven days per week, along with overtime, and there was no one to watch him. She had no extra money for a babysitter, and it wasn't going to work. She said she would if she could. I told her if I don't send him away, he's going to die from the abuse. I said he'll eventually kill us all. But she couldn't help me. I had to do it on my own or I would be in the same boat. I was forced to figure it out. I cried for days, and Ace held me and said, "Mommy, I am scared, and I'll never leave you."

After the hospital, I returned to the hell home of an apartment, and my sister left with shell-shocked forest guy and the kids. I was home with both children, and then Tiare and my aunt picked up both kids to give me some time to rest. I was down with injuries that looked absolutely horrific, and he was nowhere to be found. I couldn't see out of my eyes or walk well, and I was in pain and depressed. I felt like a failure, and I was. I was a horrible example to my children for taking shit and continuing to put them in danger all because I thought he truly loved me. I couldn't look at myself in the mirror for a long time. I had no sight that was clear, and the shame was killing me. I felt like my soul got hollowed out and I could see right through it. I was in complete despair.

A few days later, my mom came by the apartment and banged on the back door over and over. We rarely saw each other—only when I needed something. She demanded to be let in. I opened the back door begrudgingly, as she wouldn't leave. She insisted on seeing me. I opened the door and said, "Hi Mom, how are you?"

She gasped at the sight of me and started shaking and crying. She chanted over and over, "He's going to kill you, Marie! Why do you stay? Why? Where did I go wrong?"

I told her that I didn't know what to do and I was stuck. I had completely lost my way in life. I was out of options at the moment. She warned me that I needed to leave him and do something to save myself and the kids, or we were going to be in the newspaper and it'd be too late then. She pleaded for me to go get help at a rehab, to which I told her to get the fuck out. I wasn't ready and I knew that I was still so befuddled at why he was doing this to me and why there was no love. I loved him. I swear, I really thought it was love. But it was more like obsession. You only know if you know. It's a dark place to be, and I never want to return.

Jesse returned somewhat remorseful weeks later, after I had healed. He never got caught for the abuse or violating the TRO. And when he pled guilty to other crimes, any sentence that was left was gone, and they let him go. He couldn't look at me before that as it was a reminder of what an awful person he was. *Why would he want to do that? He had to save himself from the trauma.*

A huge storm was coming to Jersey and NYC. Everyone was in a panic and taking cover. Where was our family, if you could call it that? Jesse left, of course, and left me home with the kids in that apartment. He had to go get high with his friends and rally about the impending storm. When I asked what I should do, he said grab the mattress off the bed and hide with the kids under it in the bathroom until the storm passed. He didn't care that we had no water or food or electricity. He said I should be safe, as the exterior was made of cement. *Thank you, Captain Obvious Contractor Drug Derelict asshole. I am aware of that!* I wanted to shove the black roses down his fucking throat. I knew where his priorities were. His friend received a new shipment of meth and he was so excited to try it. He used Jesse as a drug connoisseur to test out the new dope. Jesse was his best feedback customer.

So, once again, I was on my own and was terrified of the storm. I dragged the mattress into the bathroom and hid the three of us under it for hours and hours. I had no way of leaving for food. So, I had my milk for Leah in the bottles and Ace ate biscuits for babies of some sort. The neighbor's corrugated metal roof was banging around, and I thought it was going to tear through the glass jalousies in the front living room of the apartment. I prayed to God to please help and protect me and the kids.

Eventually, we fell asleep, and when we woke up, we saw that the fucking hurricane had ripped its way through the Jersey Shore and most of the outlying areas near the water. Plus, heavy winds took down power lines and knocked out the power upstate for days. A beautiful hotel was wiped out and all windows were cracked, and it was a complete chaotic mess.

The storm passed, and all the while he was getting high at his friend's apartment and laughing with his dumb friends and fucking the pretty lady who lived in the apartment above. She babysat Ace and looked at me with an awkward guilty face each time I saw her, so syrupy with sweetness that it was fake.

CHAPTER 9: CHILD PROTECTIVE SERVICES

Months went by and I had moved on with my life, trying to pick up the pieces. Then he turned me in for drugs with Child Protective Services. Once that agency is in your life, they would fuck you over hard. You'd lose the kid to a horrible foster family, and they would not allow you to visit, see, or even call your own children. That motherfucker. I fed my kids, bathed them, and did my best to weather the storm, literally, alone, while dealing with all his beatings and sociopathic behaviors, and he's the one who calls CPS? That wicked bastard.

CPS began their investigation swiftly and they ordered a random drug test, which I, of course, failed. Like a slice of my sourdough toast that pops out of the toaster, that's how quickly I lost custody of them. Leah and Ace were gone overnight with strangers. Ace was screaming, "Mommy, no, not my mommy. She's my mommy and I love her."

I can still hear it ringing in my ear and the look of him lurching forward to grab me while Ms. Christine ripped him out of my hands and shoved him in the car seat, buckled him up, and warned me if I got a foot next to the vehicle, she would call 911 and have me arrested for attempted assault. I was like, *WTF, I didn't even touch you. You are stealing my children; they are all I have, and I am the only sane parent they have. Please, no!* Ms. Christine drove away and gave me the birdie. That bitch.

The next move on my end was to locate a family member that would take them on an urgent basis, so they both could be transferred out of foster care. Aunty D took both Leah and Ace. The agreement was that I would go to night classes at a nearby Methodist church for a few nights a week and work my way through the CPS process. So, I went to the classes and then started putting my life together. Man of the Korn (MOK) creeped back into my life even with the new TRO. He snuck into the house and waited in the closet. Then, he jumped out and beat the fuck out of me as he thought I was fucking a guy instead of going to the classes. I had to go to the next class with the black eye, and I remember the teacher asking me, "Exactly what are you learning if you are still getting abused by this man?"

"You're a stupid girl," she said. "He DOES NOT love you! This is NOT love. He is a sick man who needs help. Leave him. Better your life. You're smart, from a nice parent. You will lose these children forever if you think you have a future with this man."

I knew she was absolutely, positively correct. I was never going to gain custody of my children. I was beyond any terror barrier. The beatings and the terrorizing would not stop. He kept coming into my life and I would allow it as I felt I had no other way. I was trapped. I had the kids taken away on a longer basis this time, and another family member stepped in to help. Her name was Elaine, and she was Jason and Candy's older sister, and a criminal defense lawyer. She stepped up and fostered Ace in her nice Jersey home for a time with her two sons, while Aunty D had Leah. *Did I know she was my sister at the time? Nope.*

Jesse was in dark times with the kleptomania thought process. He believed it was the easiest way to take care of himself and his family. He was now onto stealing larger ticketed items that were of much higher value and risk versus the previous types of petty trinkets. And I thought that removing a large granite slab 5-6 feet long and running with it on his back to his truck was crazy. Nope, he was now going for jewelry and other items that the pretty dope dealer ladies would ask him for, and of course, this was a challenge to him. It was a test to see how far he could go. It was like the movie in which Leo portrays the pilot, *Catch Me If You Can.* It mattered more to him to feel the thrill than to actually go to the grocery store with his girlfriend and purchase food to cook. A nice family meal was not part of the package. He had shit to do. It was meth each day and night for him, and I was lucky to get thrown a bone of food, love, or rent. He wanted to be out all day and night, then pop in and drop off scraps of food, and if I fucked him, well, I would get dope. So, I would not most times, and then he would say "Be a good girl, so you can get the good stuff."

I had rights and visitation with the kids, as I was trying to do the right thing with the classes at night at the church and the other items CPS had me do. But Jesse would fuck it up each time he knew I had them and sabotaged me in not being a fit parent. CPS built their case against me each time and they were not wrong. We would be safe at home (sometimes the foster parents allowed me to have the kids) and then bam, he'd come around between 1:00 a.m. and 4:00 a.m. and wake us up as he had to shower. I lost so much weight, love, and respect for myself. The pain from Ace being pummeled was what ripped my soul into a million pieces week after week, month after month. I grew tired and finally said, "GET THE FUCK OUT!"

And I meant it. I wanted him out of my head, soul, and life. *You are out of a horror movie. Hence, Man of the Korn!* I said to him, "You are a dirty, rotten piece of shit. You are not a man, and you are not a father. You are a dirtbag sperm doner, the troll under the bridge, and the boogeyman."

He was attracted to most women, but not me, obviously. And they liked him because he had a sense of humor. He made them laugh, so how could he be so mean? We were all so dickmatized!

Why? Because of a thief in the night on dope with a dirty dick. Sounds disgusting right now. What a fucking clown. I mean, I wasn't allowed to go anywhere as I belonged in the house with the kids. So, what did I have to look forward to with these two children when I was so sad and depressed most of the time? He always made sure I couldn't do much, like dancing in a club, which was one of the most fun activities that I love—dancing. I was in dance class when I was a teenager and grew up watching *Fame* and *Flashdance*. He despised it and called me a whore and said only sluts dance.

I love all genres of music, with country being a little less. I even love jazz and the blues. One night, I went dancing and he found me. I was wearing a black cocktail dress and red high heeled pumps. He came over to the bar and scooped me up off the barstool. He left fifty dollars on the counter and said "Aloha" to the bartender. He carried me over his shoulders like a sack of potatoes and threw me in the taxi. He didn't beat me. He wanted to have mad sex because I was pretty for a change.

The shoes I was wearing came from a huge pallet Jesse stole from a loading dock. He used them to trade for dope. He had recently met a young Japanese lady that looked like she did not do drugs at all. Yet, she was a dealer and smoked a ton of meth! She worked as a medical device manager and had her own storefront with medical supplies. That's where all the dope deals went down. She loved my son Ace. Everyone did.

We were to the point that he was finally not living with me anymore, but he came by the apartment whenever he could or made me meet him at a hotel. It was a rollercoaster ride of a relationship, and sadly, our kids took the brunt of the drama. Although I had the nesting feeling come over me as I was there in the apartment, a part of me felt like I had been robbed of a fun early adult life. I wasn't a victim, yet I was. All a part of growing up, and I still could not have a normal relationship. I was confused about becoming close with people, letting them know my inner core. I became protective and guarded and didn't trust anyone. Acquaintances said I was scared and a glutton for punishment. I went from one thing to another, not really knowing what I wanted in my life. I believed I had a gap. I felt stuck. I had two children and no place to call home for them, and the type of parent I was then was not savory.

Because he could not come to the apartment and seemed paranoid to go there anyhow, he stayed away, mostly. It was safer for Ace (who was now with Aunty D again) and me. Aunty D would allow them to come over and she would let me have them alone. She believed it was BS that CPS was governing all areas of my life. She was such an enabler; however, she loved my children like her own. One night when I had the kids, he called me on the landline and told me to go outside. He said, "I am picking you up in a cab and we're going to the city. I found a nice apartment for us to rent for a while."

"I don't need be in an apartment. I have my own. I am not moving again and certainly not with you as a full-time partner. No way."

I was also settled in that neighborhood and with the programs that were helping me to stay on track to get custody of the kids. I asked in a louder tone why he had to always take it to the limit and test the waters to see if he'd get in trouble. He was playing with fire. I wasn't comfortable. He didn't like that response. I hung up on him and went back to my laundry. I love to do laundry.

He called back and said, "If you don't pack the fucking kids up now and meet me next door at the 7-Eleven, I'll come over and pull you out."

I heard the boogeyman lurking in the dark by the apartment after the call and the hair on the back of my neck stood up, which meant

I was going to get my ass kicked and so was Ace. I was forced to do what he said. I had to gather bottles for Leah, diapers, wipes, blankets, and other supplies, clothes, and a huge-ass diaper bag with a carrier. Then, Ace was easier, as he was almost a three-year-old boy with easy T-shirts and shorts, and was so used to being moved around so much in the past, that this time, he threw a fit. He started to scream and beg me not to pack up and go with him. He was afraid. He called him Uncle Jai. "No Uncle Jai, no more Uncle Jai. Mommy, please, please, please." And did I listen? No, I did not. I went with Uncle Jai with the two kids, again.

I arrived at the 7-Eleven next door, and by then, I had taken far too long, and he was losing it. I was shaking and the stuttering and heavy breathing from Ace started again. He grabbed Ace by the arm and threw him in the back seat. He picked up Leah and carried her to the front and buckled her in by him. I asked how he got a car, as it was clearly not his. I wasn't ever sure if it was another girlfriend's or stolen. Anyhow, he looked up at me and Ace in the back seat, as of course, I had to comfort Ace, and said, "You two remind me of dog shit. A pain to deal with, but necessary." *How lovely.*

Ace started hyperventilating again and I was crying again as my son was scared and miserable, and I did not know what I saw in this Man of the Korn. He was awful. He was despicable and nasty. Pure evil. I felt I could not do more, as he told me this over and over. It all went into my subconscious. I believed every bit of it, like I was being brainwashed. These are some of the things he told me:

You are stupid and all over the place—a jumping bean.

You have small tits and a fat stomach.

You are stinky, fat, and dumb.

You can't work—who would hire you?

Your mouth begs to be slapped and beaten and you deserve every bit of it.

When he was nice, he would say:

You cook some things okay.

You do good laundry.

Your housecleaning skills are nice.

He looked at me with this gnarly grimace, and then Ace would shake, and when he would stare at Ace, he would pee in his pants. I know I felt like I was. It broke my fucking heart as I was a terrible mother. *What was I thinking? I wasn't.*

Jesse said Ace and I were not allowed to snuggle, cuddle, or be near each other as we were not healthy to one another as we were both weak. He said, "You can't sleep with Mommy anymore. You are a big boy, and you sleep alone. You walk without holding her hand even if you're on the street. Be a big boy and grow the fuck up," he said to the two-year-old.

He ripped Ace out of my arms and said, "Boy, come here by me and be good. Sit down and shut the fuck up. Uncle Jai will make you into a man."

Ace turned to me with sheer horror and said, "Mommy, may I please live with Aunty D again?"

Ace got his face and mouth squeezed and was told to take that statement back. He hated that kid so much. Meanwhile, he was the sweetest and most timid boy. He continued to separate us and make me watch Leah and say, "Don't you love our baby? Why do you love that other kid so much? Who the fuck is he? An orphan from your old lover? Or is it because you still love Rathe?"

I would say, "Rathe is a thing of the past and we're done. But he does love Ace and wants him back."

I would not let Ace go. It might not have been a bad idea for Rathe to have taken him. However, that couldn't happen. He was my baby.

As we arrived in the city from the east side, I knew it was not the Hilton or some nice place. It was going to be where it was a vacation rental of someone else's apartment and would barely be decent, safe, or sanitary. He pulled into a parking structure on Beaumont Avenue, and I was like, *Here we go again.* It was the scummiest area of Tremont, literally, and we had a dark brown walk-up unit with stairs. I had a baby under a year and Ace, who was petrified that we were once again with Uncle Jai. The stairs leading up to the unit had the gap between the surface of the stairs and the bottom of the next step to walk up. He felt like he could slip through. So, Uncle Jai made him climb alone and told him he could not hang on to me or him. I was on the verge of an anxiety attack.

He may as well have put the terrorist black bag over our heads and then walked up with a, "Surprise, here is your new dwelling that you are forced to stay in until I get tired of you guys and need a whore." We walked in, and it stunk. It was a musty older unit. *Why would I want to be in this place when I had a clean, cute, comfy, familiar place for my children? Where all their toys were, and the playpen, plus our kitchen and the park.* Because Dickness Everdeen said so, that's why. And if he gave you the look, like shut the fuck up or I'll slap you, well, you looked down like Ace with the hopes you were not next.

He was smoking so much meth from day to day, as that was the juice to keep him going for the female dope dealers and their laundry list of goodies that good ole Jesse could get at the blink of an eye. The scraps came home to clothe and feed us. No more red high heeled pumps or sexy shoes. He was now convinced I needed homely clothes, as he became enraged with jealousy each and every time any man—young, old, skinny, fat, or otherwise—would even glance my way. He would become livid and then look to see if I was checking them out and the feeling was mutual. *How could I even have the energy for this when my kids were in tow and Ace and I were first to get backhanded anyhow?*

We were hyper-focused on not pissing him off as he would blow a top when he was wound up. Back in the day, the oil-based meth was pure. I know it's synthetic, but all drugs were processed for consumption. At this particular time, the Asians and the Filipinos found the recipe and had it flooded in every house, and most became addicts. Regular people were into it as it made them clean their house and be more productive at work. Then, as with anything that provides that much delusional euphoria, it's the Law of Polarity. What is up, must come down. Anyone and everyone smoked meth. Some people snorted it by crushing it and then hitting the rail, and it would burn your nose like a motherfucker. In the '80s and '90s, people lost their minds on this shit.

My plan, prior to going to this dank apartment in Tremont, was getting my act together. I was truly doing my best to be a good mommy to Ace and Leah. Emotionally and physically, I was gaining strength and had the momentum. I was searching for schools so Ace could attend most of the year and be safe for most of the day, and then we just had to ensure night was peaceful, where he could get rest and not be awoken by Uncle Jai.

The meth would make me not want to eat, and tons of weight came off instantly. What narcissistic girl would not like that? It made you feel like you could clean your entire house five times faster than anyone, your car was extra fast and smelled nice, and you were on top of the world, until it all came crashing down for all of us. For anyone who used it, it was just a matter of time before they were roped into *The Walking Dead* appearance. It made you feel like you could run forever or stay out all night, rock out all day, and then keep going until you passed out in the most unlikely place and ended up getting ripped off.

There was a time, I recall, not eating for so long that my throat muscles would freeze up and I couldn't swallow regular food, as it would get stuck in my throat and I would choke. So, I'd have to start off with soft food. And then, of course, sweets are a craving when your body is low on sugar and/or potassium. This is another reason why your teeth rot, aside from rotting your bones to smithereens. You crave bad food, you stay up for too long, you don't brush your teeth as often as you normally would, and flossing and picking becomes a thing of the past if you have too many other distractions happening. Meth rots your teeth from the inner core, as it depletes your calcium levels severely and starves you from necessary nutrition. It literally sucks you dry of all good things, and that's why when it is used over and over, the person eventually does look like a character from *The Walking Dead.* It starts with Season 1, hobbling as an extra, and then by Season 2 and beyond, you become a main character in the show. Such a sad waste. Jesse was not just hobbling; he was on the next phase of *Zombieland.* Not quite SAG-AFTRA!

In the apartment, Jesse saw the look on my face and was livid. He didn't like the judgy smirk. It was absolutely ridiculous that we had to be in another apartment paying rent, when he could have used that to pay another few months of our rent, so we wouldn't end up homeless. However, he was selfish to the core. There was an underlying reason as to why he took us there. So, he would once again get us set up and then say, "Oh, I have to meet up with someone to sell this thing or do a deal so we can eat tomorrow."

And I'd say, "What? When do you plan on coming back?"

No answer. He'd be gone with a joke, so he would make light of the situation and then leave for hours again. It was so pathetic. I'd put the kids to bed and then sit there with no dope, as he would never share. Then I would watch over the balcony to see if he was coming home. I never saw him. As Eminem says, "Window pain, not pane." I would be watching for his bicycle and then all of them looked like his, and I would be imagining him coming home and just wanting to love me. Never. I would leave my post on the balcony for a bathroom break and then Houdini would pop in and say, "Daddy's home."

He'd be in a good mood with money and dope, and then we would be told, "Oh, now we're going to the Hilton or Sheraton, or somewhere nicer for dinner."

This time, he didn't want to go anywhere. He was basically teasing me with the dope, making me beg for it, and then I'd question where he went all night. He always smelled like he just took a shower, as he claimed he was a sweater, and he truly was. However, where was he showering at? And why not come back to the hotel, apartment, or my house and shower, right? Because he was unfaithful and was a sick-ass sex addict on tremendous amounts of meth.

The day after we checked into this place with him, where he left me all night, he told me, "I am taking you and Ace with me tomorrow on a field trip. A girl I know will watch Leah as well." I asked, "Why do we need a sitter for Leah?" He said, "You never know."

I said, "I am not going anywhere. I want to stay home with the kids."

He got a strange look in his eyes, and I could tell he'd been up for too long, and he had the jealous vibe. *Here we go with his imagination that turns into a psychotic delusion that I am the bad girl.* I opted again to stay back and just be with the kids. He refused and said, "No, I want you to come with me."

It was broad daylight, and we all accompanied him to this condo where this known big dealer lived, along with many others. Apparently, she was the Dragon Lady. Dealers were like rock stars in their own right, and they had a time where they were famous—the woman or man on top of all else. And all it took for that role was to have the best dope in town. You were a HERO if you had the good stuff. Grade A Wagyu, as we said.

This woman probably can only be described as a cunt. A full-blown, fat cunt from the gnarliest land of cuntiness you've ever experienced. Her name was Miss M.

We arrived on the top floor and the elevator opened. I looked down at Ace and was horrified by the terrified look on his face. I wanted to run out of there as fast as I could, but honestly, how would I do that when Jesse had Leah in the carrier that sat in the stroller, and Ace was not allowed to hold my hand anymore, as "only pussies hold hands"?

We walked down a long corridor, and it was open, where you could see the street below. It was higher up than we were used to. We approached the door, and he rang the button with a soft knock at the end, like a little boy scout signal. *How fucking cute, you slime bag!* Ace started hyperventilating and ramping up to a full-blown anxiety attack, with tears rolling down his face. He was in so much internal pain—you could see it externally. I was crushed and I started crying, asking Jesse why he felt the need to torture us and involve us in his bullshit scheming life. Why couldn't he just leave us alone?

He told me in a very psychotic voice, "I will throw you over this balcony in front of Ace if you don't shut the fuck up, cunt."

A guy with a tweaker grin opened the door. It seemed like he had not washed his face in months, as if the acne abscesses on his face were ready to jump out and bite you. I hoped one wouldn't burst onto me and my children, as I have the worst case of OCD with certain triggers that light me in a heartbeat! This clown allowed us entry, like we were walking into the Taj Mahal. *Give me a fucking break, you idiot with no life. Well, who am I to think this way when I am the Queen of Losers walking into this shit?* There was a slight foyer, and then I saw an end table, a large lamp, a glass coffee table, and a balcony with sliding doors directly in front that led to the other side of the building, where you could see tons of other buildings through the glass. The carpet was soft but not new, and clearly had seen a lot of traffic. The sofa also looked like it was once nice, but was worn from many asses or bodies that had laid on it. The lighting was dark and yellow. I saw a kitchen in a nook area to the far-right with white appliances.

The one feature that stuck out in my head was the wood jalousies in the kitchen. *Why would anyone install that material in a room that has grease and other scents from cooking?* Anyway, we were not there for a materials lesson about what had been installed in said unit of this drug dealer. We were there to talk about dope. I turned to look at Jesse and he pushed me in the door, where we were forced to sit on the couch and wait, like we were sitting at a doctor's office. He told us to be quiet and not make a sound as he parked the stroller at the side of the living room and removed Leah. She was hot like him and sweaty.

He took her and brought a diaper, wipes, and her scarf-like blanket. He opened these large closet doors with a bedroom behind it. I could see that there were two king size beds in the room behind those doors. I could also see a female laying down with a pipe in one of her hands. She was wearing white jeans and a turquoise blouse. She had dark hair to her shoulders, with a middle part, and she had a mini blowtorch in her other hand. She lit up the pipe and it caused a glow on her face. She was fucking ugly as shit! She had pockmarks on her face from previously picking the meth sores on it, she had no makeup on, and dark purple natural lips from smoking too many cigarettes. She looked weathered. I was in shock. The first thought that ran through my mind was, *He would rather be with this chick than me and the beautiful kids? This guy is definitely smoking too much meth. It has clouded his own vision of reality.*

The windows above her allowed the sunlight through, but the curtains were drawn. There were mirrors along both sides of the beds and a large nightstand in the middle made of shiny white lacquer. It was all white, with this '90s type of paisley hodgepodge shit. Her toes looked ashy with corns on them. She was gross, to say the least. Jesse laid my sweet-smelling baby next to her, and I sat up and told him, "I'll be back. Can you bring my baby out here?" He turned to Miss M, proceeded to lay the blanket down, and put Leah by Miss M. He closed the door and apologized to her for my behavior, and excused himself while he closed the door slowly. Ace was panicking and squirming all over the couch, and was now crying loudly and having a fit.

Jesse looked at me and said, "You make me sick."

"I make *you* sick?"

Wait a minute, you fucking low-life motherfucker. I was boiling inside, and this was the last straw. I had let my life spiral out of control, and he was calling me the sick one? I had had enough. The burning bed in my mind was an understatement.

Jesse grabbed Ace by his arm like he was a scooter, where he still had bruises from the week before. He dragged Ace into the kitchen by the wood jalousies. *What is with those slats of wood?* No screen, no barrier, and they were loose inside the track. The ugly bitch of a drug dealer was still in the room, cuddling *my* baby. I was so upset and wanted to go kick her ass. However, Leah was not in danger. But Ace was.

I quickly started to look at my options of escape, and there were none. He had literally mapped it out, and there was no way out for us alive. I ran over to where Ace was and said in a calm voice, "Please, Jesse, leave him alone already. He is clearly traumatized, and he is innocent. He didn't ask to come here, and he just wants to play in a park like a normal kid and not be subjected to all this unnecessary bullshit."

I got slapped across the face by that Popeye-sized hand and went flying, landing on my back where the carpet met the linoleum floor in the kitchen. The drop below Ace was probably six stories high or more. We were so high up, and my little boy would die if he was pushed through that set of wood material. I crawled to my feet. My head was hurting so badly, and I was spinning. I was so dizzy. I am barely 5'2". The kitchen was small, and you could barely fit a round table in there. He pulled the table and blocked me from entering the kitchen to save Ace. Ace was standing there at attention, and just kept saying in a chant, "Yes, Uncle Jai, yes Uncle Jai, I promise."

It was his go-to response when he was about to get his ass kicked. He looked at me and I was screaming. That pock-face bitch did nothing except sigh loudly, as if I was getting on her nerves. She did not render aid. No one called the police. I prayed to God, *Please, Lord, help my son and do not let him go out those windows, as I'll go right after him.* I was beyond hysterical, and Ace was still standing there hyperventilating and huffing in front of Jesse. I screamed for Miss M to come, and she didn't move from the bed. I didn't hear a sound. I screamed for the dude with the pimples, but he didn't move from his station. All I had was Jesse, who was beet red, profusely sweating. And now, it was war. He turned to me and said, "You know how to ruin a good time, bitch."

I was the next person up, and he moved the table and grabbed me by my hair, then grabbed Ace by the arm again and dragged us both to the area between the sofa, coffee table, balcony, and kitchen. He railed on me and started banging my head into the floor over and over. I started seeing stars and it was getting echoey and quiet. I felt myself slipping away and yelled in the most stifled scream, "Ace, don't leave me! Ace, I am so sorry!" And then, blackness.

I awoke to Ace under the end table against the wall by the lamp cord, where it plugged into the wall. He was shaking his head and nervously raised his index finger to his lips to express, "Shhh, Mommy" in a whisper. I crawled slowly over to him and then touched his arm where I saw the bruises. His arm felt hot to the touch. I felt so nauseous and had a huge lump in my throat. I scanned the room, but didn't see anyone. I could hear Miss M giggling and Leah cooing, as Jesse let out a funny shout. He was playing with the baby, his side salad, and laughing after he just traumatized a two-year-old and the mother of his children—well, one of them. As I was under the end table with Ace, I accidently hit the lamp and it tipped over, crashing to the ground.

The laughter in the room stopped, and all I could hear were those heavy closet doors opening at once. I got a solid look at Miss M and gave her a look of despair. She smirked at me as if I deserved every bit of it and then shook her stupid head and continued to touch my baby. I tried my hardest to put a pillow in Ace's arms and said to him, "Shield your head and heart, son."

I pulled myself up, which took all my might, and swung at this fucking clown with a large ceramic object from the '70s that was on the coffee table nearby. I missed and clipped his ear. He started bleeding all over the carpet. I saw Ace push his face into the pillow and just held it there. I grabbed him and was running toward the door and Jesse caught me by the back of my hair and yanked me backward. Ace landed on top of me as we were falling back. I landed on my back and was once again out cold.

My eyes blinked and I was on the floor again. I heard a lecture coming from the hallway. It was Jesse kneeling in front of Ace, screaming, "You fag! You little crybaby fucker who needs to suck on his mommy's tits to feel better and can't be a man!"

Poor Ace was beside himself. That soul of his was tarnished forever. Miss M was smoking her pipe, blowing smoke out, and playing with Leah, tickling her now. I rolled over and said, "I am calling the cops, and I am taking my kids away from you."

I stood up. I was in so much pain, but also numb to an extent. I picked up Ace and grabbed the stroller, looked the bitch in the eye, and snatched my child from her. Then, I spit in her face.

I said, "You are a cunt, and you hit every branch of the ugly tree on the way down, inside and out. How could you witness this and not help another human, and one of your gender, to boot?"

She was stone cold, laughed, and rolled over like she was at the beach in Cabo. Now that is a motherfucking, stink-awful cunt.

Jesse seemed in shock that I was still standing up and picking up all the belongings carefully, not to forget one piece of evidence that I was there in that scumbag, dragon lady's condo. I put both my kids in the double stroller, and I left. I felt strong, exhilarated, and free. I was on top of the world! I was barely hobbling and pressed the elevator button. How else was I going to escape? The bell rung and

I stepped in. The doors were just closing when the Popeye hand shoved them open, and he got in the elevator with us. Ace looked up for a minute, and then put his head down in pure defeat.

I was white as a ghost. The wind had escaped my powerful sails and the world went dark once again. I was silent. I could not believe that he had the fucking audacity to jump in that small space with those he just tortured for hours.

The elevator doors opened and he grabbed the stroller just as I got Ace out, and told me that I really knew how to be a buzzkill to the fucking party. I was following with Ace holding my hand. Jesse looked down and I told him that he could fuck off. My son was two and he could hold my hand as long as he felt like it. He looked at me as we walked into the apartment and dragged us onto the couch. He then said he was going to cook dinner as he hadn't eaten in a while, and we should sit down as a family and enjoy time together. *Are you fucking kidding me? Will an angel walk and toss him off the balcony, right out the front door, please? Headfirst.*

He then told us that we needed to shower, so we were tossed into the bathroom. I undressed and saw all my bruises. I looked at Ace and started sobbing. I washed Ace up and then myself. Then, as I was combing my hair, he came in and said, "You both should rest. I'll take care of the baby." He put Ace in one room alone and told me that I must sleep in the master bedroom and give him space. I told him once again to fuck off. I grabbed Ace and headed toward the main bedroom. Jesse screamed at me to leave him alone, coming to me and ripping Ace out of my arms. He shoved me in the door, and I landed on the bed across the room. I tried to open the door, but he put a chair under the knob and shoved a table against it. I was trapped. He didn't give a fuck about me or anything else. Ace was exhausted and had no energy to hyperventilate or cry. All he wanted to do was sleep, I would imagine, and curl up next to his mommy. I heard him muffling Ace, and Leah wasn't crying at all. She was cooing and just cruising. I stared at the wall made of CMU brick and planned my escape in my mind as I tried my best not to drift off into a deep sleep.

I woke from and to a horrible nightmare and realized I had to pee. I sat up and looked around to orientate myself. I did not see anyone or hear a sound. I tried to open my door and it worked. He must have moved the furniture. *Thank God.* I went into the bathroom and peed, but did not flush the toilet. I was trying to tiptoe and see what was happening. I saw that Jesse was sitting up in a lazy boy but was passed out cold from being up for days. I walked down the hallway and opened the door to my son's room. He was on a twin bed with his back turned to me. He had the same CMU brick walls with a window he couldn't see out of as it was close to the ceiling. There was something near his head, a food-like substance. As I got closer, I saw it was clearly vomit. He had barfed in the bed. I turned him over and he didn't look well. He was whimpering, shaking, and scared. My stomach had a knot, and I felt the worst anxiety in the whole wide world. I looked closely and knew he was hurt in some way; however, I was unsure as to what degree. He was trying his best not to cry, that poor baby. I lifted him up and he started wailing in pain. I screamed, and all I could say was, "No, no!"

The monster woke up and I said, "Oh, I am taking him to bathe. He must have thrown up."

He blocked the door to the bathroom and said, "It's early in the morning, go back to sleep. I got him."

I blocked him and said, "He's my kid, I got this."

I pushed my way to the shower stall before he could. I still remember how dark and ugly the tile was, a dirty brown, with larger grout lines and small two-inch squares. I turned on the water to distract from the sounds of Ace whimpering and starting to hyperventilate, and I was signaling him to remain calm and be quiet with my index finger against my lips. I slowly removed his shirt, and I could not help but start to cry. Of course, dickhead was right behind me, and we both saw it at the same time. A black, blue, red, and dark colored raised shoulder against his pale skin. He looked down and I lost it. It was just horrible, and I couldn't stop crying and screaming. Jesse was even panicking, realizing that we both were not in good shape. So, he almost wanted to hit us, but realized my son needed medical attention and I was near losing my mind.

He pushed me aside and grabbed Ace. I forced my way in between them and snatched Ace from him. I went into the shower and washed him of the puke and urine smells. Jesse was struggling with me, trying to control the situation, and I was on the most desperate prayer of my life—*God, please help me get away from this psycho to save my child from this agony. Please. I promise I will be done.*

Lo and behold, I was gaining confidence as I packed up my belongings that were important and headed for the baby while I was on the phone calling the taxi. I was changing the baby's diaper, packing the milk and diaper bag—a routine I could do in seconds if I had to. Then, psycho came back with the fucking big-ass hand that is ten times stronger than me and said, "You fucking cunt, you're not taking her anywhere."

I very sternly held back the tears in a calmer fashion, and said, "I have to take both of them for their immunizations today, remember?"

"Not with her, you're not. Reschedule it."

I went on insisting, and he started ramping up. I looked into Ace's eyes and saw fear and desperation, and I decided I must get my child to medical attention now. If that meant leaving Leah, his daughter, who was not abused by the man of the Korn, devil incarnate, then the vibe was to leave her behind and return with the police. I couldn't sit there and argue and cause my son to risk his life, the baby's, or mine, for that matter. It was on and I made my decision. I packed up and agreed to play the role. I told Jesse that he was right, and I'd call him later once we were done with the shots. He grabbed my arm and said, "You're not going to report this to the doctor, are you? Make sure you tell them he had an accident and fell down the stairs while you had groceries in your hand, and it was too late by the time you got to him."

I said, "Okay, no problem. I'll see you later, okay?"

I left and walked down the stairs in a bit of a moderate rush and saw the cab approaching. I thanked the Lord and asked him to help get my son and I to safety and to forgive me for leaving Leah temporarily with this crazy motherfucker. I looked up and he was holding her like a caring father, waving, cradling, as if I was going to the grocery store or the park and returning to those open arms. But he had a warning in his eyes that I had seen too many times prior. I looked at the cab driver, who asked me, "Are you guys okay?"

I said, "No, Sir, we are not. Please take us to our apartment at this address."

I hugged my son and held him so as not to further squeeze him, and we were out of the city heading toward our place. It was the longest cab ride home in my life.

I walked in the door, examined my son again, dressed him in new clothes, and then got dressed myself. I called Jesse's mom and explained what happened. I proceeded to tell her that I was on the way to the hospital to get my son treatment and his immunizations. She did the usual, "Aha, okay, I am sorry to hear this."

She always forgave him and invited him back into the house momentarily, only to allow showers and food to eat for that day. She wouldn't give him cash anymore and understood he was off-and-on the benders and supporting his family with drugs and thievery, regardless of his construction and painting skills. *I mean, why work, in his mind, if you can steal and deal your way to the top?*

I hung up the phone from Mrs. Grandmother who couldn't care less and called another cab. When we arrived at the pediatrician's office, I got out of the cab and made my way into the lobby as best as possible. I saw the security guard and smiled. He looked at me and was about to ask if I needed help, but out of the corner of my eye, I saw Jesse lurching forward. He was in midair to my right side in an instant.

I screamed, "Help us, please!"

The security guard was already enroute, racing over even faster. He yelled at Jesse to stay the fuck away from us. When he approached us, he knelt down to Ace, who was hyperventilating, and whispered, "Little boy, what happened to you?"

Ace lost it, dropped his sippy cup, and put both arms around the security guard, saying in a stammer, "Please help me and Mommy. We are in danger from Uncle Jai."

The guard lost his shit and walked over to Jesse, grabbed him by the shirt, and said, "You son of a bitch, you better stay the fuck out of my territory, or you'll wish you never met me."

Jesse was sweating and had an attitude. He told the guard, "Fuck you, clown, and stay out of our business."

The guard then said, "Son of a bitch, you made it my business."

He told Jesse to wait outside and then called 911. I was begging to be allowed upstairs to the doctor's office, as we were going to be late. He told me that he was sending over an escort. I attempted to explain quickly what had happened and he told me, "I have seen and heard enough. Please wait here, ma'am."

The escort arrived and we headed into the elevator to the eighth floor. I had the worst anxiety ever. I was so disgusted with myself. *How can you put your children in danger any further and the same old speech that sounded like a song on the Fleetwood Mac record I sometimes play over and over. Rumors. I am just secondhand news or have you ever dreamed...*

The guard and cronies tried to apprehend Jesse, and of course, the clown got out of their grip, then took off, yelling, "She's a fucking cunt and her son is a pussy."

The elevator doors opened, and the escort guard told me, "After you, Marie."

Ace, who was trembling, walked with me to the check-in counter. They made us sit down and then we were called in at once. The medical assistant was staring at us, and I told her what happened. She was in shock and stopped writing, and then excused herself. The pediatrician entered the room immediately thereafter. She started to examine Ace and he winced as she got near his shoulder. The hyperventilating started again. She informed me that he would not be receiving his immunizations on that day and stated that she would be having the nurse call for an ambulance. We needed to get him to the hospital as soon as possible. I swallowed hard and asked her how bad it was. She told me straight up in this disappointing tone that I was all too familiar with.

"Marie, you have a severe situation that you must remedy or a member of your family, including yourself, will no longer be here. You must save this boy of yours as he is in pain and traumatized."

She further stated that she hoped I would be turning in the father to the authorities and for me to take shelter where I would be safe.

The doctor called the nurse and medical assistant into the examination room with us. She instructed them to contact the nearby Children's Hospital and alert their emergency team of his arrival. Then she said to bring us in through the back door with a police escort. She turned to me and said, "I am not administering his vaccinations as he is in severe pain, and this can wait until he's in a better state, both physically and mentally."

I looked down in embarrassment and shook my head over and over. *I am an epic failure as a human being*. The disappointment in myself and the fact that my child was hurt due to me not being able to keep him safe was pathetic as can be. I was a total fucking loser.

I took the elevator down to the lobby, stepped out, and went to the pay phones in the hall. I contacted Rathe. I told him where I was and gave him a minute download of the current predicament and recent events leading up to it. He was literally packing his bag while he was talking to me.

"I am on the next plane there and I'll see you at the hospital."

I took a deep breath and released a sigh, then broke down in tears, as no matter what had transpired between us, he was still loyal and on his way with no question in his mind. He needed to be there for Ace. All I could recall was the time they both encountered each other for the split second and Jesse fleeing, leaving me in that house to be beaten for hours in only my striped Ralph Lauren T-shirt.

I turned to head back upstairs and retrieve my son to wait for the ambulance. I grabbed my bag to exit the hallway and there comes Jesse again. He goes to tackle me, then grabs my arm. The same guard comes from behind him and puts him in a choke hold, then tells me to run for help. I ran up eight flights of stairs and arrived panting, when I saw Ace. He was so happy, yet in so much pain. I will never forget that look. Confusion, pain, and love all at the same time. I held him and promised him that we were getting help and that Daddy was on his way from the country. He smiled and closed his eyes to rest. He felt safe and was looking forward to seeing his dad, Rathe.

I was in the emergency room and Ace was receiving care. The doctor came back with the X-rays in hand. He looked at me and seemed a little put off, as I did not look like a drug addict or a mother who doesn't take care of her children. I was told this by many people I met during that time of my life. The doctor proceeded to say that Ace's collarbone was broken and must heal. He must be safe and away from further trauma or harm. He told me that the staff would be moving him upstairs to a new unit, where he'd stay for an indefinite amount of time until he could recover in a safe home. He said that the bones needed to fuse together, and it would have to happen in a controlled environment there. They set us up in a room that had a cot-type twin sized bed and cage crib. The crib was where Ace would remain for the next couple of weeks, and his cage crib would be secured with a lock only the hospital staff had the access and authority to open and close. I felt like I was watching someone else's life on screen in slow motion. The room was a solid distance from the nurses' station and near the stairwell. It had its own bathroom, so I was set to be there day and night, in safety, while my son's bones fused.

I got us settled in and waited until Ace was asleep in the cage crib. I then turned my attention to the plan on how I would get my daughter back. The police took our statements, and I included the information for them to retrieve her from the last known address, where we were at that awful apartment. It turned out he was gone and had checked out early, according to the owner. I had no knowledge of where my daughter could be and was so worried. It also dawned on me that he didn't have her with him when he attacked me at the medical center.

I called the babysitter, who was a hybrid of Jesse's whore and my babysitter. I had a gut feeling that my daughter was with her while he stayed at his friend Lance's house to be the meth aficionado. She answered the phone, and I told her not to tell him what was happening. She asked about Ace, and I told her what Jesse did. She was somehow shocked. He was awful to Ace. No shocker. Disgusting pig.

I looked over at Ace and he was still hyperventilating even while he slept. I teared up and told myself that this must stop now, and we must put Jesse away to teach him a lesson, as well as to keep us safe. Ace was my tail, my connection of love, and I broke all trust with him by allowing a man to pummel us on a regular basis. The PTSD was on fire, and the whore on the phone told me, "I will get your daughter back for you."

Now I was shocked. I hung up the phone when she did and fell asleep with the heavier part of the phone in my hand. I was sitting in front of the doorway that led to Ace. I would protect him as best as I could.

I woke up to Rathe tapping his cowboy boots on the hard hospital floor. He asked me how the fuck we opened this cage. I looked at him in a daze and I was clearly fucked up looking, as he just shook his head and walked out toward the nurses' station.

Rathe introduced himself to the charge nurse on duty and advised her to open his son's cage. She was dumbfounded and asked who he was. She checked him out and he was issued a bracelet that would allow him access to Ace and all areas of the hospital that the public would not be able to. He returned to the room, threw his backpack on the floor, and sat down. The nurse entered and opened the cage crib. Ace opened his eyes and saw his daddy for the first time in a long time. He was so relieved, so happy, and said, "Hi, Daddy-O, I was wondering where you were."

I started balling, and Rathe laughed and said, "I could feel you needed me, Ace."

They were reunited and Ace was safe. I drifted off to sleep on the twin bed in the corner as I knew then that we were safe and no one was going to fuck with us with Rathe there.

In the morning, Ace was awake, and it was time to feed him. Rathe and I switched shifts like we did when he was an infant, and it was his turn to sleep while I took over. Ace was in pain and the nurse administered Motrin in his IV. He had a small piece of wood to keep his arm straight and those animal printed hospital pajamas that made me depressed. I cried again. I was sleep deprived and probably strung out as it had been a minute since I got high. Rathe woke up and told me I should go back to the apartment to shower, pack a bag, and return with items from home so Ace would feel comfortable. The staff advised Rathe to accompany me and that they would watch over Ace. We promised we would return and, of course, Ace was upset seeing us leave. But we assured him we would be right back, and he seemed more confident that Rathe was there—like all was back to normal, like when we all lived together. But my daughter was still missing. The police had not located her yet, and I was a train wreck at that point. I had a vision that Ace was never going to be the same again, and this was just the beginning.

As the news got out into the family, one member came forth—it was Tiare, my sister-in-law. She came to the hospital and was our outside support system. She looked for apartments near the hospital for as soon as we would be released, once the bones fused. So we were looking, and Rathe was going to pay for it. I had my apartment; however, it was not safe, and I was advised by the authorities and CPS that Ace was not to stay there until the heat simmered down. On the daily, I was informed by CPS and the police that they were doing their best to locate Jesse and our daughter, who was still missing.

One night, I decided that enough time had passed, and I wanted to go home, shower, wash clothes, and then return to the hospital in a cab. I left and Rathe knew I was safe, so he stayed with Ace. I just wanted my baby back and to be at home so I could straighten my life out and be alone with my children as a single mom. I had a purple and green blanket that my friend sewed for Ace, and I used it at the hospital to give me one comfort from home. It had the scent of both kids. I sniffed it all day long. Rathe had this blanket over his head and was asleep. I was not there. It was late into the night and pitch-black outside. The story I heard from Rathe went like this, and the nurse who witnessed the incident vowed Rathe told every bit of the truth…

The hospital floor was similar to that of a department store. Ace's room was approximately 100 feet from the nurses' station, and it was right next to the stairwell and far from the elevators. It was the only room at the end of the hall with no neighbors. Rathe said he couldn't sleep and chose to have the blanket over his head for obvious reasons. He was baiting Jesse, as he wanted him to try and enter the hospital so Rathe could kill him. The police said if Rathe beat the shit out of him, they'd look the other way and render aid before Jesse was near death. A few kicks, punches, and backhands is what Rathe was envisioning and looking forward to.

Rathe was facing the door and saw through the blanket the running shoes and hairy legs, with no voice to announce himself. From one convict-criminal-derelict to another, this was to be a showdown, the first of its kind. The hooded figure ripped the blanket off Rathe's face and wham, Rathe jumped to his six-foot self and grabbed Jesse by the neck, dragging him out of the room, so as not to further put Ace through any more trauma while he was healing. He pulled the body where the nurses' station could see with their cameras and witness the incident. Jesse jumped up and darted for the other side of the hospital. Rathe ran after him with the cowboy boots. It was nearly 2:00 a.m. Rathe grabbed him by the shirt, pulled him close, and put his solid fist right into his face and neck. He was going for the Adam's Apple next, then the 1-2 I'll kill you move. Jesse went flying, scrambled up, and dashed out of the hospital. Rathe couldn't chase him with his bad knees.

Because this was a serious incident, the entire security plan had to be revamped, and we had to have a guard sitting in front of Ace's room 24/7. His new pseudo name was Allen Lee. He had new tags printed and his chart changed to "Name: Allen Lee." The staff said to get into the habit of calling him Allen in case any of the other patients' families gave us up to him. We found out that he was downstairs paying people off to get intel on us. Like Ace was not confused enough at this point. Poor baby.

After two long weeks and bones still not fusing, my ADHD was on fire. So, while Ace was napping and Rathe was sleeping, I took respite in visiting the floors with the children who had cancer or terminal illnesses. Back then, the staff knew me and the situation and didn't believe there was any harm in reading and making the other kids laugh. It was my way of giving back and feeding my soul. It felt so nice and was a break from being depressed in Ace's room. One girl was bald and looked forward to seeing me outside her door.

One day, I got a call from the nurses' station when I was on the ninth floor where the NICU was, and they asked for me to be sent down. I was scared, thinking Ace was in trouble. I ran down the stairs, and I was back to see that Ace was still sleeping and so was Rathe. I ran to the nurses' station, and she asked me to sit down. A female emerged and asked me to follow her into a room. She closed the door and proceeded to tell me that the police had found my daughter, but Jesse got away by jumping off the first floor. The police could not locate him, and he was still at large. I was not surprised.

I was told to contact a number on a card. It was the CPS office. They indicated that Leah couldn't visit the hospital due to her age and the nature of the situation. They then proceeded to tell me that my Aunty D was willing to take her in and that she would assist with the facilitating of said child visitations. I was so relieved. My daughter was safe! But the boogeyman was still on the loose and I would not be able to concentrate as he was always in the back of my head and mind, and one step ahead of me. The police came in and asked if I wished to press charges, and I said yes. They took my full statement weeks later and I was also filing an extension to the existing TRO on file. Another nightmare of court appearances and bullshit.

Rathe and I picked up Leah and were allowed to take her to Aunty D's. We took her home to clean her up, packed up her items, and then headed over. Rathe looked over at me and said, "She has black hair. She could be mine."

I looked at him and told him it's not possible. He turned and said, "Fuck you."

We left and were on our way to where Aunty D lived. We visited for as long as possible and Aunty D said that she didn't want to get us or her in trouble by having us there for too long.

Rathe rented an apartment for us in SoHo, as Ace's release from the hospital was in two weeks. His bones fused and were staying put, so that was good news for us all. We all moved in after the release, and it appeared to be us as a makeshift family. It didn't last though, as Rathe got a call from upstate. He was offered a long position at a multi-family complex in Albany. He stated that we could stay until the lease was up in a month and that he had to head back to take this assignment. He felt bad that he was leaving me and Ace. My sister-in-law brought my daughter to me as often as she could. Ace was a mess and became withdrawn again. Rathe awoke early in the morning and left before we all got up. I called him that night and he said he had to work and if I was around when he got back to town, he and I would connect. I never thought that would be the last time I would ever speak to him or see him again.

I was looking in the mirror a month later with two children next to me. It was time to return to my own apartment. I was barely on state assistance and needed to get my life on track. I lost my housing voucher from another county when I left with Jesse to go to the city. We were not deserving of that anyhow. I knew I kept a clean house, and I was capable of finding a job and babysitters. I started to slowly believe in myself. During this time, Aunty D would come over to my apartment to babysit and spend time with Leah. It was so helpful. CPS ordered me to attend the classes again at the nearby church with the same instructor. Oh boy. Aunty D would arrive after work, stay the night, and Leah was so happy. Ace was too and he felt so safe. The undercovers were looking for Jesse on the daily, so our home was the last place you'd find him, and we loved every minute of it.

As a family, we were focusing on getting into a program with the children and then assistance so that we could start over, and eventually, I could get a job to put both of them in daycare, preschool, and then regular school. Jesse was on his benders and kept on stealing anything and everything, plus God knows what else.

The narcs were watching our house for when he would appear and he never did, thankfully. By that time, I had consumed so much meth that I myself was now a full-blown addict. I had the freedom to be with others who had the dope, and I had no issues getting it for free.

CHAPTER 10: METH, METH, AND MORE METH, PRETTY PLEASE

Because I was no longer with Jesse and had some freedom for the first time in a long time, I started to venture off and meet people outside of my immediate circle. This was when my life took even more twists and turns. It was one location or adventure after another … until it wasn't.

Mr. B entered my life from another man I met at AA. He was Asian, short, crafty, great with math, and had tons of cocaine and meth (aka ice)—the good meth. I didn't like coke anymore. It was expensive and I wasn't productive on it. I felt more accomplished on ice. Mr. B was a hands-on dope dealer to all walks of life and had a connection that seemed to be the best in the Metro area. His dope was the best meth and coke the street had seen for over the last decade. He was generous, loved women doting over him, and had guys that did everything for him, from butler duties to finding whores he could fuck for a week. And while, yes, I was very sexually active at one point in my life, I always really wanted just one main squeeze. This guy did not turn me on, even with excellent ice. He was what I had to deal with in order to be high on the daily. I mean flying high like a kite soars and whips back and forth.

The reason I needed to be high all the time? You don't feel the guilt when you are in that state of mind. The failure of non-motherhood was under my skin. My kids were once again taken away from me. What I longed for was someone who would just love me and think I was golden. I never got it … not then anyway. Mr. B should have been Mr. D for devil incarnate number two.

In the era we were in, pagers or beepers were the form of communication. I can still remember Mr. B's number to this day and not my own. Those goofy but handy contraptions would buzz on people's hips—whether they were clipped onto their pants, with or without the fancy chain, or hidden in their pockets. A page would come in and you had to look at the number, then the number would have entered codes in the message, which was then used to communicate about dope and other matters. *Seems like Morse code, huh?*

We would use landmarks to find the hotels or the dope meetup. We were a band of gypsy drug addicts on the run. We never stayed in one place for longer than 24-48 hours. We (whatever gang of friends I was with) moved around like The Mamas & The Papas on tour, from town to town, state to state, and then back around in another loop, but zigzagged, to throw off the narcs. I can tell you every alley, side street, hotel, what streets are one way and ones that have parking lots that used to lead to other streets, and walls that could be scaled or otherwise. These were the days of rottenness. I can still imagine all of it over the years, imbedded in my brain. All we did was get high, put on makeup, get dressed, get high again, then leave the house at night to get supplies, visit others, smoke more meth until the sun came up, and then wash, rinse, repeat day in and day out. Months went by, and I had not seen nor heard from Jesse.

I was living in the same apartment at the tail end of the tenure there and had people over all the time. I met higher-end drug addicts with larger amounts of meth that could cover my habit, and I was able to make a few bucks by putting people in connection with each other. A friend named Mrs. L got in touch with me and indicated that Jesse missed me. She became the messenger. I was furious with her and told her I wanted no part of that man anymore. He almost killed me and my son, and I was finally healing and living my life.

One night, we were getting very high, and my phone rang. I picked it up, but no one said anything. There was just heavy breathing. Mrs. L called me next and asked if she could pick me up so I could go over there and hang out. I agreed, and she arrived about an hour later. She drove to her house in the country, and we set up the party area. I went to the bathroom, and when I came out, Mr. Black Roses was sitting there shaking his leg, so his dick was bouncing up and down, as he was trying to dickmatize me. There I was, believing her that we were about to party amongst just us, and here was the psycho that was now sitting right across from me. I wanted to spit in his face.

"You've been busy, haven't you?"

I didn't reply. *I don't answer to him anymore. Fuck this clown.* I looked at her and started to leave. He stopped me and handed me a large bag of dope.

"Since when?" I asked. "Since when do you give me this much dope? It must be fake."

"No, I've been busy as well. Here you go," he said, as he handed me the dope and a necklace that he started putting around my neck.

"I'm so sorry, Marie."

Of course he was. And of course I fell for it again. Yes, I did. He made me laugh, and once that happened, my heart and mind were mush. *Drugs truly cloud your fucking judgment, all the way.*

We were now in the third hour of smoking a ton of meth. I was cleaning Mrs. L's kitchen that was full of dishes and making my way around the house to clean everything else. She was happy, as she knew by the end of this bender, her house would have been deep cleaned by a tweaker and she could let it go (her style, not mine) until the next time Jesse and I used her pad to get high and fuck. Yes, fuck, as that's all he ever wanted to do was fuck, fuck, fuck.

Mrs. L told us that it was going to be a full moon, and she had to gather all her stones and crystals to recharge them in the blue moon bath. She was ethereal and a strong indigenous spiritual person with a massive meth problem like all of us. We would become storytellers and get so deep into the weeds. We became part-time philosophers with tales from the crypt. *Blah, blah, fucking blah.* Jesse loved it there because there were so many ways to easily escape from the cops. She had a forest park-like setup beyond her back door.

One time, we were up all night long into the morning, and Jesse decided to shower inside. I went outside to shower at the same time, as she had a beautiful lava rock waterfall set up that was not quite finished but still really nice. I'd get bitten by bugs all the time when I was in there, but it was cool for sure. I returned to the dope table, and he was sitting there looking stressed and irritated and started to lay into me for no reason, asking why I showered out there and who did I meet in the dark to fuck me in the few minutes I was out there. *Here we fucking go again.* I am not sure if she called the narcs or they just caught up with him, but they were in that town looking for him at every public area and he got wind of it. She smiled a knowing smile at me, and I was like, *OMG, she set him up for me. Well played, Mrs. L. Solid as can be and so manipulative! Amen, sister.*

He heard cars and screamed at me, "You're a cunt!"

He bolted out the window with no screen, jumping at least ten feet below, and was off and running as the sun was coming up against the water. He escaped to a location where they film a ton of movies by the water with a park on the inside. We were following him according to his orders via three-digit codes on the pager. Mrs. L was laughing and saying over and over, “You can run, but you can’t hide.”

He managed to get the balls to jump into the murky swamp water and hid from the helicopters circling above. The narcs wanted him so badly that they too jumped into the water after suiting up. The divers surrounded him and trapped him with a net like a big fish. They caught a big one that day! I was finally free from the devil incarnate number one! And he was set up by his own friend, who loved Ace to death. She did that for that little boy to get that motherfucker back for what he had done. She did what I couldn’t do and I loved her for it. I could make a break for life with the kids, and I won! *Won what? Nothing, that’s what.* I was a loser as well. I was just as bad as he was. I didn’t realize then that this would not be the final encounter with this man, but for the time being, I had freedom, and I wasn’t going to get my ass kicked that day or raped or watch my son being beaten again. I was safe and I could return home to my own apartment that I paid for and decorated, maintained, and kept as a place that my kids could visit.

I took his car, or as we called it, the Green Hornet, but it was damaged, so I took it to a garage in the city. Unfortunately, I told the wrong person about it, who magically knew his cousin. What a small, pathetic world. The cousin told him in prison, and they plotted against me by locating the car. They stole it from me at the garage and the guy who owned it was paid off and said that since it was not only in my name, it had to be released to the Power of Attorney. *What POA? Who had that?* Well, it was his cunt cousin, the huge dragon lady drug dealer at that time, who took my car and I was without a vehicle and was about to be homeless, to boot.

I continued to allow this rollercoaster of a life to toss me around, so I couldn’t see what was coming. I started to see other guys. I met up with Mr. J, who was also dating my brother's ex-girlfriend, unbeknownst to me. He was a cop's son, and he had a brother who was normal, with a family and a dentist. This druggie guy had strayed off from the family values and was one of the largest new dealers in the nearby hood, with good dope. I thought—*Well, perfect, this works out as we can both help each other. I can be his friend, and he can be my supplier. I can perform menial tasks around the house and hope I don't have to fuck him for the current and forthcoming dope.* He was handsome but awkward and uncomfortable with himself. He looked like Joe Manganiello's brother.

We were friends, but he started to look at me differently. He asked what I liked to do, and I told him that I liked fancy dinners, drinks, and dancing. He agreed to the earlier, but no dancing for him. I got dressed in the cocktail velvet piece from the dope dealer that I had for a while. Those dresses from her came in handy. We went to the Windows on the World restaurant, and they gave us a killer view in a corner. It was always such a beautiful atmosphere. I was seated first and felt like I was in my comfort zone. After dining with a multimillionaire and a billionaire there, this was a piece of cake. *This falls in my wheelhouse, bitches.* I was in my element, loving life at that very moment.

The waiter came over and Mr. J was clearly not feeling it, but he saw I was and so he dealt with it. I placed the order in proper succession, and he smiled, impressed and dumbfounded. He told me that he was surprised and had seen another side of me that he liked but was also intimidated by. I was this gypsy, couch surfing addict on the street, who lost custody of her children, and had no family that could or wanted to be a part of her life, but I cleaned up well and could hold my own in a fancy restaurant.

I told him about my adventure as an English teacher in Japan and how my father worked on the motion pictures, so I had been around Hollywood stars and acting all day long. I had been taken to nice dinners and cultured by living with the elevated gangsters. *Big deal, right?* He was not from a bad or absent family like mine. As we sat there, I realized that it doesn't matter who we are; drugs and the squalid that crawl in that realm do not discriminate. They will take a poor or rich soul and turn it into a dark one quick, no matter how smart, sharp, or ahead of the game you think you are.

It was also on that night that he felt the need to distance himself, as he believed we were not aligned. That was actually the last time I saw him. He kissed me goodnight at my door and said, "I had fun with you, and I am glad you became my friend."

He also said I looked so pretty. It was a weird goodbye. I never said goodbyes, and that was it for us.

Many trolls continued to enter the realm, and I was deep in the culture of fuckery. I was sewing my oats to make up for lost time. I was done being captured, beaten, and made to hide in the corner. For all that time with Jesse, I never wore makeup or anything pretty. I was shunned, suppressed, shushed, and felt super ugly. I looked in the mirror on the daily and didn't see beautiful. I saw pain and scars, hurt, and no love. But then I realized I was a fucking free woman. I could do whatever I wanted and hustle my rent, meals, and dope with no guilt whatsoever. On the downside, I was under even higher scrutiny and was told by the state that I wouldn't get the kids back easily again. They told me, "We know all that you do."

Well, I guess the devil incarnate number one was giving them all the information they wanted on me from jail. "Rat Fink Fuck" is what that was. The state advised that I needed to attend a drug rehabilitation program. So, I went on a quest to locate and hook up with every large dealer within a 100-mile radius of me. I was successful, of course. I gravitated toward only those who had the money, cars, dope, and shopping allowance to shut my loudmouth up, and then they got high in peace while I was out buying up the world but going nowhere. My self-image at the time was high. I went on a serial rampage of dealers. I had to survive.

Around the same time, I met an older woman with a wisdom vibe. She was twenty years my senior and yet, it was like we were best friends from years past. She was a hairstylist and was trained with both archaic and modern methods. Plus, she had her own huge salon on the property. Her parents and other family members resided there, but all in different units. It was a compound of relatives.

She could service two people at a time plus two could sit and wait in the same area, with the door locked. *What did we do in there?* Got super high. She had a bathroom next door for us and her customers to use. It was the coolest fucking setup. She had her mom's house that was massive, multi-units, parking fronting the building, and then a driveway that led to the middle house. Behind that were the other smaller units, plus the salon. And it was all protected and shrouded, so no one could infiltrate. It was safe and they felt like family. I loved it. We used it for all the wrong reasons. She had these twin poodles, and she made this scrambled egg dish with onions, Patis, tomatoes, and garlic with oil in pan. Sometimes, she would throw spinach in it for me. She and I became so close as I introduced her as my aunty, and everyone assumed she was. We acted like each other and were on the same frequency. We used her home as a base to shower, sleep, get beautified, and hide a ton of fugitives and drug dealers. This was a dark crowd.

There were two guys we knew and both were okay looking. One was a sports guy, who turned to the dark side. These were not my typical type of people I wanted to be around, but it seemed like I always somehow gravitated to them. *Geez, maybe the Italian in me and from the Calabria in my blood. I don't know, as my grandfather was the Chief of Police there and had run-ins all the time with the criminals and the other team.* These people were scary. I started to spend more time with these folks as another Asian dealer guy that was helping me didn't quite like that I wasn't putting out, so he took the next whore that was available. "The Tease" was my nickname—not whore or slut, as I truly didn't want to fuck anyone. All I wanted to do was get high and run far away from those who tried to control me. So, it became my reputation—the tease. She doesn't put out and takes all your shit and runs. I was a productive eye candy gal, who could cook, clean, wash laundry, take care of pets and humans, drive to perform errands, and look hot 24/7 while I did all that.

Okay, so these two boogeymen were exactly that. During that time, I was also being fostered by another bizarre person, who was my druggie friend's father. He was the ringleader manipulator. We had a name back then used on the street, "Kadafi." We were subjects to these Yoda-like guys that would come up with schemes and use some of us who had nothing else going on. Well, desperate times call for desperate measures. I was being used by this family in tandem with all this other shit happening. So, this man was gross and weird, but he knew all the players. His name was Mr. C. He was the father of a son who performed all his bidding, and they wanted to rent me to the tall Asian guy in the city, who was a larger dope dealer. The guy wanted a clean girlfriend and asked if he could have a regular companion who was cultured to eat in nice restaurants, travel, and be a professional arm candy piece for a few months. It was proposed to me, and I agreed to do it. The Chinese guy with the beeper was doing his own thing and I honestly wanted a different gig. While this was going on, I got mixed up with a guy whose father owned a mortuary, and he and his brother would steal jewelry off the dead bodies.

The other guy was a scary motherfucker that I knew killed others. I had no proof and still do not; however, he was the worst—you could just feel the vibes. He was handsome but a cruel and heartless person to the core, and all he wanted to do was fuck strange, pretty girls, while his woman was beautiful. *Go figure.* Both of these men liked capturing me and hiding me at hotels, houses in the wilderness belonging to their close friends, or trailers in fields with no way to escape. One of them sliced about six inches of hair off with an X-Acto knife on the backside and tossed me across the room. They both would apologize and wanted me with them only on some days. It was so fucking weird. I was glad I never got too tied up with these two guys. Once, they left me in the middle of nowhere with strange people in the mountains and I had to fish my way out by walking to the main highway, and when I got to a gas station many miles away, I was able to call a cab and head into town to meet up with Mr. C, who was trying to sell me to the tall Asian for a few months.

I arrived at the condo in the city and Mr. C had me enter, locking the door behind me. No one else was there. He fed me dope and an hour later, he forced me to take my clothes off and raped me. He was disgusting and his semen smelled rotten. I ran to the bathroom and barfed. He came in there and wrapped me with a sheet and didn't allow me to shower. He wanted me to sit in it and remain stinky, with his jizz all over me. I was disgusted, repulsed, and freaked out. PTSD took over, realizing I was now a slave who was paralyzed. He hit me and I fell into a sleep of exhaustion. When I woke up, he was sleeping. I grabbed my clothes and ran away to a nearby friend's house in the city. I showered for a long time. I couldn't get the stench off of me. I was permanently scoffed and stained. I cried myself to sleep and when I woke up, I went on a five-day bender. I was already vulnerable enough—just in time for the Devil Incarnate to get released from prison.

Jesse was released into a work furlough program, and he found me. He told me that he heard that I was involved with a group of killers, rapists, and other unsavory people. I thought—*Is this really coming out of this prick's mouth? Seriously?* I wanted to punch him right through the phone. He asked if I could meet up with him at a hotel in the city, so we could rendezvous like we were old sweethearts. I was so tired of this guy, and while I should have hung up, he suddenly didn't seem so bad compared to the lunatics I had been hanging out with since he was taken away. I met that motherfucker and had hours of sex with him. He headed back to the work furlough program, and we lost touch again. I was on my own, continuing down this destructive path.

I was back with the guy who wanted to rent me like I was a Blockbuster DVD. We will call him Mr. L. He asked me to meet him at a restaurant. When I got there, I told him that the deal was off. I was raped by the sick fuck father of who was trying to rent me. He got upset and called the rapist and told him that his line was cut for what he did and that he better apologize. *Are you serious with this scrupulous honor amongst thieves code? Get the fuck outta here!*

But this guy met up with me and told me he was sincere, and he would pay me direct for the companionship only. I asked what else was involved aside from that and he told me nothing, except going shopping and to restaurants with him. I agreed—an unwritten agreement between two parties. He didn't expect me to cook or clean, but I did it sometimes anyway. I moved in with him with very few items. My belongings were in public storage again, as I had gotten asked to leave since I could not pay my rent for two months. So, all my shit went into storage, and I was stuck with very few items and storage I could not afford either. All my pictures and memories were in there from years past.

I was at a condo with massive square feet overlooking the water, a nice master bedroom, and all the comforts of luxury living for being a friend. I could do this, no problem. It was a decent break from the all the other BS. I did notice that this companion, who soon became a sex partner as well, disappeared and didn't come home at times, even while looking like he wasn't dressed to go anywhere. I was perplexed and continued to watch.

It was now around 30-40 days after my move in, and this guy was definitely up to something, according to my spidey senses and intuition of the CSI vibe. I followed him one day after he said he was going to play golf without his clubs. He took the elevator to the seventh floor. His apartment was on the twenty-third floor. I saw him go up to a door and use a key to enter. He had access. *Weird. A second apartment. A rental? What could it be?* He then disappeared for hours. I ended up ignoring it and continued to play the game. And we continued with our elevated and comfortable lifestyle. He visited the seventh floor quite frequently. But I let it go for the time being.

A week after the last disappearance into the seventh floor unknown unit, I decided it was time to knock on said door. *Why the fuck not?* He was paying me and he wasn't in the unit as much, and I was wondering—*Is he using me to watch the dope? That clown! Am I the security guard for your fucking drugs? Are you kidding me? I was meant for more than that!*

He left to go golfing for real, and I knew it was all the way on the other side of town. Plus, he'd have dinner with the guys, then drive back. And by that time, it would be near bedtime. I had plenty of time to investigate. I got dressed and knocked on door 714. *Wow, the number on a quaalude, Rorer or Lemmon 714s? I had gold earrings given to me by a guy that said "Rorer 714" in the shape of a pill and they were dangly earrings. Too bad they were torn out of my ears. My left side has been called a pizza slice or a self-mutating scar. Nope, it was Jesse James tearing my quaalude earrings out of my ears, so he could pawn them to feed himself meth and not his children food.*

I was perspiring and nervous. I crossed my heart and said a prayer to Mary, St. Anthony, and the Universe. *Please bless this encounter. Amen.* I knocked on that door with the lion door banger with ruby-colored crystals, so at least this person must be classy. I was now excited—*Who was this mystery person?* I was waiting for a response as I heard music inside faintly. I then heard someone walk to the door and push up against the peephole. It turned dark, and I could see someone staring at me through the door. There was a long pause, and then the door opened.

There was a woman standing there in a loose cotton see-through house dress. She had orangish hair that was supposed to be red, except for likely using a box formula from the drug store. She had all her teeth. They were not white, but decent, and she looked like she was Korean and Caucasian. She had a blowtorch in her hand. Music was playing in the background (Alanis Morissette, to be exact), and she had a lighted area that I could see over her shoulder—a jewelry making station, from what I discerned.

I scanned the apartment, and it appeared to be clean and organized, yet she had the essence of Korean food, as I remembered that from my friend in middle school. She had a fluffy Persian cat jumping from sofa to sofa. I started to introduce myself and she said before I could get a word in, "Are you the girl who lives on the twenty-third floor with Mr. L?"

I was shocked and intrigued at the same time. "Yes, I am. Marie is my name; nice to meet you."

She opened the door wider and said, “Come on in,” like we knew each other from when we were kids.

I was baffled and in shock. She knew we resided upstairs. So, now I was thinking—*it must be his cousin, sister, or a relative.* She invited me to sit down at her station and offered me a Coke. I replied, “Sure, and a water, if that’s okay.”

I monitored her as I didn’t want to have a kernel of Ricin get magically put into my beverages. I took a seat and asked, “So how are you guys related, by the way?”

She said, “He fucks you and I am on a part-time side salad basis. That’s what this is.”

The look on my face must have been priceless. I mean, I almost choked on the Coke. She said, “In a year, when he can trust you, you’ll have your own apartment like me. Maybe we’ll be neighbors, and I can move up to the higher floor. It’s nicer in there, but I am happy here.”

I was beside myself, having difficulty wrapping my head around the fact that this blunt-ass bitch was seriously just talking to me over a soda like it was a matter of fact and totally normal that she was having sex with the same man I was, she was getting paid like I was, and we were neighbors in the same building. So, she was his current fling. She had been to the unit, and obviously fucked him in that same bed I slept in. He visited her and fucked her in the seventh floor apartment, and then came home and snuggled with me in the twenty-third floor apartment? Wow, this was a way different setup than what I was used to.

The issue was that I was a selfish person, and I would compete on some level with other humans. So, this was a serious issue for me as I was super, uber, hyper selfish and that meant I was not receiving all the dope, money, and extracurriculars I thought I was. How naïve of me! At that moment, she was asking if I wanted a piece of Korean fried chicken with rice balls, and my head was spinning. I looked at her station and politely declined the food offer. I asked her what she was making.

"I am setting stones I received from a friend and teaching myself how to set them like a jeweler at a wedding ring shop would."

I was partially impressed, but the other side of me wanted to slap her, but I couldn't. She was actually quite cool, and I thought to myself—*no wonder he fucks her as she's Miss Fucking Positive!* She was teaching herself to set rubies, peridots, and diamonds into white gold (apparently, her favorite material to work with). *Weird-ass shit.* Of course, I asked her if she could mount my Aquamarine stone that I'd had for a long time. Well, she had the size that fit my middle finger, an 8. She told me, "Look at this!" as she slid it on my finger, telling me that with that stone, it would look so rad!

I started laughing and found that she was a kindred spirit of a friend, and obviously the frequency was there, as we both fucked the same guy in the present tense. And we would be continuing, apparently, if we went with HER plan. *Do I ever follow another person's plan? Not if they are on the other side or in this type of weird dynamic.* I do know how to navigate in awkward situations and play the role if I need to. And that is exactly what I did.

I was playing the role with her and Mr. L on the twenty-third and seventh floors of the Manhattan condos that have open walkways. I continued to have dinner and mingle with Mr. L when he was up for my flavor. He treated me extremely well, like a princess. I also visited my new neighbor when I knew he'd be gone all day and night. But I didn't like to share—not a man, clothes, or dope, even if I was being paid. *Hell no! So, what did I do? Retaliation, of course!* My plan was in full motion.

I was deep into planning my departure and leaving with a bang. This was weeks after I found out about her and I was having a difficult time keeping my head on straight. Of course, it didn't help that I was up for days on each bender, making myself go psycho over this arrangement. This guy had it all laid out—he cherry-picked girls that were brought to him by other drug addicts he could trust. They vetted, like any recruiter would, and then would select the finalists of the group applying, more like who was selected to be tossed into the ring. He had them STD tested, so no surprises there, and he used protection when he did have sex. To be honest, he fucked her more than he did me. I guess I was still known as the tease, or someone who doesn't wish to have sex as often. By that time, I had been fucking raped so many times. Who could have normal sex after that, and with the fucking built-in PTSD?

One night, a group of gangster dealers came over. They were a mixed bag of Irish and Italian guys. They were a crew of one capo (lead guy), and the rest were associates or wise guys. They were larger in size and not the sharpest knives in the drawer. The lead guy was borderline smart, but these were not authentic wise guys like the ones that take care of you. Those were goodfellas and they don't deal drugs—they were at the top of the food chain and gave orders. These were guys that Mr. L had as his Joe Boys. They were discussing a deal, and I was in the kitchen acting like I was minding my own business. After all, I was only a dumb whore who believed he really liked me and I was his main dish. *Wrong.* So, I continued to act like I was in my own world, and this circle of guys were talking about the pick-up point, the amount of cash associated with the deal, and the drugs that needed to be stashed at a safe house in town. They were lipping with all this data that could have put them in jail. Such dumbasses.

I got asked to serve them beverages. So, I broke out the ice and started making cocktails and pouring wine for the capo—a Piedmont

Nebbiolo that was from 1983. Nice color and taste. *Now, let's get on with the plan, Marie. Play the role, you got this.* I found out when the cash was being dropped off. A guy would be delivering it to Mr. L's apartment at 11:00 a.m. on Sunday before the afternoon game. Perfect! The boys would be watching their football and I would be gone, laughing all the way to wherever I was headed, which was out of there. I was not going to be sharing and mingling with these sick fuck people that arranged it all and lived like that. It took the spontaneity out of it all! I planned my route and did it all in my head as I couldn't write it down … for God's sake or mine. I had memorized the times, date, and scenario in my head. I was manifesting in all the wrong ways and for all the incorrect reasons.

Sunday came and it was football time … and time for my escape plan. I showered, got dressed, and looked at all my lovely clothes and gifts from Mr. L. I was sick inside that they would not be coming with me. I would be on my own again and I had to leave only with the clothes on my back. I was never returning, as I would be dead if I did.

I served heavy appetizers because, well, guys get tired, lazy, and overly comfortable when they're eating well. It would be just the right mood to pull a quick one while they got sloppy on a Sunday watching football. *Nice, Marie. Good so far.* I had all my jewelry on and my best outfit with athletic shoes to wear on the way out. The doorbell rang, and I ran to get it. Mr. L said, "No, I got it. You relax and keep serving. You're doing a terrific job."

He was commenting on what had gotten into me that day, as I was being Martha Stewart with all the delicacies, and the guys were loving me like I was their little sister. I saw that the guy who was at the door was the guy who said he would be arriving at 11:00 a.m. on Sunday. He was here. He had a red and black barrel-type duffle bag that was stuffed full. Mr. L put it in the bedroom on the bed and then lit up a joint. Shortly, he was stoned. Lovely. The rolled cigar of Indica that was baited was taken easily, and Mr. L was not paying attention. He forgot everything when he smoked weed, including the duffle bag that was on the bed that he fucked me on and probably thought of Miss T as she said she was wicked at the blow jobs.

I left the kitchen and walked by the crew. They were relaxed, happy, and enjoying the apps with the game on. Their team was winning. But I was all about what Marie had planned in that brain that got called stupid by so many men in the past. I headed into the room, opened the sliding door, and saw the duffle bag. I hid it under my jacket on the chair next to the bed and went into the bathroom to pee. Mr. L walked in ten minutes later and found me at the mirror applying lipstick. I turned to him, and he told me how pretty I was and that he was happy I was in a good mood. He then grabbed me and tossed me on the bed. I was taken aback, and it was foiling my fucking plan. He was giggling and acting out of sorts, as the weed was good. Grade A fuck-you-up shit. This was backfiring on me. *Oh no.* I laughed and played the role, as I was trying to see how the fuck this was going to work with him on top of me and rolling around. I moved to plan B that I had just envisioned in my head two minutes earlier. I needed to start a fight, so I could leave in a bad mood.

I sat up and said, “When were you going to tell me about your friend downstairs?”

He was absolutely befuddled. He scratched his head and said, “What in the world are you talking about?”

I started to grab my jacket, but then I realized that the bag was underneath it. I couldn’t put it on! I must follow through. I anxiously grabbed my jacket, felt for the duffle bag, and put it under my arm. I moved toward the door and said, “I am very disappointed in you, Mr. L. You betrayed me. And with someone less pretty. But I heard she can suck a dick pretty hard.”

He choked, and there it was—guilt by unintentional admission. He was shocked that I was in on his secret, and he was upset that I was questioning him while the crew was there. I told him that I was beyond upset and that I was leaving for an hour to go to the nearby department store, and I needed cash. He looked at me and grabbed his wallet, handing me $1,000 cash. He told me to go get whatever I wanted and then return. He promised not to see her anymore. *Liar! They all fucking lie.*

"I believe you and I want to leave to clear my head."

I started for the door and the capo said, "Marie, come here and give me a hug for that fantastic plate of meatballs. They tasted just like my nana's!"

I put the jacket-wrapped duffle bag in the kitchen by the bread. I shrouded it and walked over to the capo. He said, "You're the best, Marie." He gave me one kiss on each cheek and a bear hug. I laughed and told him that he was the best! I walked toward the kitchen, grabbed my jacket- wrapped duffle bag, and was outta there! *Bye Mr. L, bye friendly neighbor who gave great blow jobs, bye capo and crew. You were absofuckinglutely lovely. Hope the game went well! Enjoy those meatballs.*

I was running with the duffle bag wrapped in my jacket and my heart was racing a thousand beats a minute. I looked left and right, then I spotted a 24-Hour Fitness. I dashed in and went to the bathroom where I cleaned myself up to look presentable. *Back then, you could do that.* I tucked the duffle bag under me, and I put the jacket on the outside. I knew it looked dumb, but I had to conceal the red stripes. I put my hair up in a bun to disguise what I could and then stepped outside. A huge guy walked up to me, and I thought he was one of them. I took a step back and he asked me if I needed any assistance with joining the gym. I declined graciously and laughed nervously.

I told him he's so big that I thought he was a football player for a minute. He blushed and said, "Let me know if I can help you with the store as well."

I asked, "The store?"

"Yes, we have all this new gear that came in and we have items in your size."

It dawned on me that God clearly wanted me to survive this latest episode, and so I said, "Hey, dude, take me to the clothes and sports bags!"

He shuffled me to the clothing racks and where the gear was. I had a guardian angel. I found a sexy, yet fitness-based shorts set outfit, a baseball cap, and a new duffle bag that was a square shape, plus new shoes and socks. He was smiling from ear to ear as he said he made 9% commission, so he was obliged to fulfill the requests with the best customer service. I asked if I could change, and I headed to the dressing rooms. I removed the tags and put on my new wardrobe as it was all that was left to my name. I unzipped the duffle bag and realized that this was the first time I was seeing the contents. I nearly vomited when I realized that I was in more trouble than I thought. Not only did I get the cash for the dope, I also had half of the dope, and someone else's money who invested in said dope. *Oy, Fucking Vey Vey!!! What have you done? And "you better run, you better hide" as Pat Benatar sings!*

I calmly took out all contents of the duffle bag and transferred it into the square bag. I shook the duffle as hard as I could. You never know—OCD. I folded it up and placed that in the square bag. I rolled up my used clothes with the bag and pulled out $500 in cash and tucked it in my new sports bra. I pulled the door open and walked to the register. The total came to $428.93—professional shopper, obviously. I thanked the guy and asked him to call me a cab. He said, "No problem." I waited and the cab showed up around the corner. I bailed and asked the cab if he could drive me to New Jersey. He looked at me and said, "How much, lady?"

"Will $700 do?"

"No problem," he said. I asked him to take me to a nice hotel and he recommended one on the beach. I also told him that I needed to make one stop at my mother's house first. He agreed and said, "I'll take care of you, lady."

I pulled up to Mom's and was panicking. I went to the pay phone at the store up the street, which I hadn't seen in years. I called her and she picked up on the second ring, as always. "Hello?"

I don't recall exactly what I said as I was tired, in shock, full of anxiety and remorse, and excited all at the same time. I had outsmarted gangsters and mostly I paid Mr. L back for being Dickness Everdeen. I told her that I was alive, and she was freaking out as she honestly hadn't known for a while. I had run away from home at fifteen, and saw her intermittently at funerals, family gatherings, and when I had the kids in my custody. She was asking all these questions, and I told her to shut the fuck up. I didn't have time, and the meter was running in the cab. I asked her to bring a paper bag and a knife with her downstairs. She said no to the knife, but yes to the bag. She came down her stairs in tears. I got out of the cab and walked toward her. I asked her to reach in my bag, as on the way there, I had counted out $5,000, and figured the rest was for me. But when I got there, I decided to give her $7,000, as I knew I would only smoke it if that was in my possession.

I asked her to take the bag upstairs and to hide the money in her safety deposit box until I asked for it back. I paid her $1,000 to keep her mouth shut and she agreed. She asked me how I got the money, and I told her it was from gambling. She bought it as she knew I had visited the illegal Chinese gambling halls in New York above restaurants that were typically hidden through laundry facilities and down long hallways and then through stock rooms, and bam, you're in the "Asian Atlantic City" of the underground. I got into the cab, and I offered to pay another $100 if he left me alone and didn't fuck with me. I told him I was carrying, and he told me to sleep, and he would wake me up when I got to my destination. I closed my eyes, telling him, "You touch me or come near me, I'll fuck you up, and if I don't, someone else will and I already know where you live." I drifted into a deep sleep in the back of the yellow Buick with the cool AC on.

I woke up to bright lights shining in my face. I was in the cab, and we were pulling up to the porte cochere of the hotel. I wiped the crusties out of my eyes and pulled my hair back again in a bun. I looked down so no one could see my face and put my cap back on. I double checked the entire back seat of the cab and moved all the cab's personal effects in and around, so he could see I was not fucking around. He laughed and held the door open for me to exit at my own time. He looked at me and said, "You're a nice-looking girl. You belong in a safe place with nice people."

I pulled out his cash and handed him another $50 on top of the $100. I said, "That's for minding your own business and getting me here safely. I appreciate you."

He was happy and told me that he wouldn't have to work all week long and he could be with his children. That warmed my heart. I grabbed my one bag, headed to the front desk, and checked in. He told me he even made a reservation for me under Carol Smith. I told the front desk clerk that a hoodlum took my ID, and I was Carol Smith. I shoved $100 under the document she had me sign and I grabbed the key.

She said, "Have a pleasant stay."

I headed toward the elevators and saw a general store, bar, and much more. I was happy, as I could easily live there temporarily until the heat died down. In the morning, I would locate the hair dye, as it was time to go blonde. I felt the beach vibe come over me! I opened my room door, and it was fabulous! I threw my square bag on one of the beds and went to the balcony, opened the door, and said to myself—*Mr. L, that's the last time you'll ever fuck with a female like that.*

I was in the lobby of the hotel purchasing two boxes of this Clairol shit that said I would be blonde, or close to it. I had zero to lose. So, I bought it, as well as a pack of Benson & Hedges Menthol Lights, and some snack food. I got whatever hygiene products I needed, as well as clothes from the resort shop. It was time to turn on the tourist image. I bought a wide-brimmed hat and a bikini. I was in the process of doing my hair when I realized I forgot the scissors. I needed to cut the hair a bit as it was a dead giveaway. I went back to the same store, and lo and behold, I saw the two guys that had rented me to Mr. L!

I ducked and one of them saw me and came right around the corner. He grabbed my arm and said, "Drop the scissors, we got you." They forced me to walk with them back to my room. *I am fucked, so fucked.* They tossed me in the room and told me that I had to pony up, as they heard I'd ripped off the boys. I told them I didn't have a thing. My mom had the money, and I had hid the dope in the hotel room where they would not find it. I only had $2,000 on me and they didn't know that either. It was in the safe. They told me to open the safe and empty my shit out. I followed their lead, and told them I didn't take it. I left because he was fooling around on me. They didn't believe me, as the bag went missing, and only I was there. I claimed it was a setup, and Mr. L ripped off the capo. They believed me and asked if they could have some cash to get back to the city to test one more time. I told them I was broke, and some guy took pity on me as I was crying in Atlantic City. I ask them nicely to leave and they did. I played the role to save my fucking life.

I was now checking out of the hotel in my resort clothes and blonde hair. I was no longer safe there, and what an idiot I was to go to Atlantic City, and of course, this hotel. *What kind of criminal was I? Not a good one.* I took another cab and called the Chinese guy with the beeper and asked him if I could stay with him until it was safe to go back home. He invited me to the hotel of the week, and this time it was a business one near the airport. I moved in for the next few weeks, and we were traveling to other Marriotts, Hiltons, and the like. I was the new tagalong to the recent entourage he had. My funds and dope were running out as I sold most for pennies on the dollar so I could live off it. I was now down to the scraps of dope and funds. I still had money with Mom, and I knew she would hold it for me. I realized I had no positive outlook on life. I was just in survival mode. I backed into my safety net, as he would support me as long as I told him what he wanted to hear, made him feel like a God, and cooked for him. It was easy dope and shelter until I was off to my next gig.

It was nearly two weeks later when it dawned on me that I was late once again for the rent. I called the landlord, and she told me to check the notice on my door. My heart sank, and it was time to face the music. I got nauseous and I ran to the bathroom to barf. It must have been from the stress. I let him know that I was departing the airport hotel and it was time for me to return to my place. He offered to get me a cab, and we disconnected, until we meet again. I was off to my place, and when I arrived, I had a Notice to Vacate on my front door.

CHAPTER 11: PUBLIC STORAGE AND FRIENDAMIES GALORE

I pulled the notice from my door and walked in the door. I looked around, and even though it was full of bad memories, there were good ones that overpowered the negative. I was embarrassed, and yet, not surprised. I supposed my neighbors would throw a party once I was gone, and I decided to bow out gracefully and not fight the system. I hired guys from the street who moved my items that could fit to my mom's, and the rest went into public storage. This was tough. It was out of the way and back then, the storage facilities were different and not air conditioned. My entire life went into that 9x9 locker again, and I closed the door and knew it would not come back to me. I paid the rent every month until I could not, and the entire storage was later auctioned off. All the family pictures, furniture, personal effects, and my entire house from the country was gone in the blink of an eye and sold to the highest bidder. But it was only stuff.

I started to feel bloated, tired, and like my mid-section was enlarging. My tits started hurting and I was reminded of the feeling that was all too familiar. *How the fuck did this happen? OMG!* I did the math and counted backwards to the one and only Jesse! Another child from the Man of the Korn. *Good Lord. Have I not learned? And how did this even happen?* I thought it couldn't be his, and when I once again assessed, it could only be him.

Despite how the story sounds, I am not as much of a slut as you think I am. A derelict, sure, but on that scale, I was leaning toward not. I made an appointment, and the doctor told me I was for sure, 100% pregnant. Jesse was in prison, and I was not sure what I was going to do. I was being evicted and had no funds, except for what was at my mother's. I tried to work at the Hyatt as a cocktail waitress, and it didn't work out as I was not earning the tips to survive. I was perplexed as the days went on, and I knew I had to move soon, or the sheriff would physically remove me. That was not going to happen.

I was invited to stay with the wife of a dentist that I used to sell drugs to. She was crazy, but always had a house and car. She was never homeless, as the spouse paid her bills. She was perfect, controlling, and I knew I would be safe. I moved in and was living at the top of a hill in Jersey overlooking other nice houses. I was bored to death and pregnant. I was stuck there all day and eating my life away.

I couldn't believe that at twenty-three, here I was in the same situation, pumping babies out like a puppy mill. The dentist's wife made me comfortable and told me stories of Pearl Jam and how they were going to be huge in the future. I hung out with her even though we did not have much in common, as she would skydive, play golf, smoke meth and coke, and then go surfing. She was what we call an athlete drug addict. I, on the other hand, was not into any of that then. I wanted to be high so I could hide the epic disappointments of non-motherhood. Soon thereafter, I met a lady at a drug dealer's house, and she invited me to stay with her, if I became her Joe Girl. I agreed, as it seemed like a lot more fun than where I was. *What a mistake that was.*

I was somehow always pregnant in the country, so it seemed appropriate and made sense to move in with the drug dealer couple and become their housemaid. She was a female narco—in her bed all the time with red lipstick and red hair. She bossed everyone around, and her boyfriend was mean, abusive, funny, and would get kicked out every other night. No one wanted to be her assistant or housemaid. She was crazy. As I cooked, cleaned, and did their laundry, they fed me marijuana and shitty meth. *Subpar crap. No Breaking Bad cooks or clear ice.* Instead, it was the one that smelled like a stink flower burning. I guess it was good that it turned me off because I didn't smoke it, which was better since I was pregnant. I laid off the dope and I gained weight, rightfully so.

The couple was full of drama and the relationship was clearly abusive. He crawled up the side of the wall and used the tether pole to escape when she pushed him out the second floor window. We lived in a two-story house with people who resided downstairs and also used meth. She supplied the entire neighborhood and next county over. She did not look like a dealer, other than the crazy amount of traffic to the house. I was the butler and maid, and I talked to people while they waited to be called into her bedroom to do the dope deal. She smoked with all of them and just sat in her bed and got high as a kite all day and night long. She slept like a normal person and ate. *Weird as fuck.* She was on it for years and she still had all her real teeth. I was being worn down with the "Right this way, sit down. Would you like something to drink or eat? Wait here. She's busy, come back," and blah, blah, blah. The job sucked. I wanted to get high and forget what a loser I was. But I did meet a whole new community of drug addicts.

This pathetic life went on, and I was a mess. I felt the depression creep in, as I had nowhere to get sober on short notice and have my baby, not to mention that my ex was still in prison and didn't give a shit. So, I went to see him, and he told me there wasn't shit he could do for me in there. By that time, I was close to having the baby and I was trying not to do dope, grasping at straws. I ran into an old friend, and he asked me to cash a check for him and he would pay me for it. I was elated, as I could get the fuck out of their house and try to start on my own. Of course, the check was not valid, and I ended up with him across the street, me going to jail with a belly. While in the cell, I got water from the sink and splashed it on the floor and yelled for the guards. They came running in and I told them that my water broke.

They called 911, and I was quickly whisked away to the nearby hospital. Once there, I fell asleep, and I awoke a few hours later to an Asian lady standing there in front of me. It was the bitch, Christine, from CPS. I couldn't believe she was in my hospital room! She told me, in no uncertain terms, "I am disgusted with you as a parent. Mark my words, you are losing this baby once it is born, and I will be so happy to take it away from you."

She was such a cunt. I wasn't a victim to her, and she said she didn't care about what happened to me. She was heartless and kept true to her word.

When the hospital saw I wasn't in labor, they released me. I walked to a friend's house and got high. I walked nearly twenty miles, and I looked like a crazy lady. I ended up at Eddie's brother's house and he listened to my griping and told me I was the craziest bitch he knew. He took pity on me and fed me. I was grateful. Then he lectured me in a nice way and advised me to clean up my act, or don't. Pick one.

It was morning, and I made my way to a guy's house who had just inherited his mom's estate. We connected, and he offered to let me stay there. But before I could settle in, the couple I'd been helping called me back. They needed help setting up for a party and asked if I could return. I agreed, helped with the setup, and at one point, the woman asked me to pick flowers from the trees. That's when it happened—my water broke.

On the way, I took a hit of meth. I was pregnant, and I knew better. Her friend had offered it, and after staying sober for a while, I caved. As soon as I did, regret hit me hard. "What have I done? I can't do this," I thought. The woman and her chaotic boyfriend, who was tied up in some dangerous stuff, offered to drive me to the hospital. I refused and asked if I could take a shower and head back to the house instead. I was panicking, so I drank a cup of vinegar, hoping it would somehow cleanse my system. Fear set in—I already knew CPS had warned me they'd take my baby.

When I got to the hospital, the staff immediately told me I was in labor, and the baby would arrive soon. I was wheeled into the delivery room, and there was a mirror in the closet and scrubs on a nearby chair. As I closed my eyes, the nurse told me it was too late for an epidural or any pain relief—I had to go through this naturally. The pain was intense, and I was screaming, trying not to focus on what was happening around me.

Suddenly, the narco boyfriend put on the scrubs, pulled the mirror out, and came over to me. He said something that made me scream, and his girlfriend exploded, yelling at him. They started arguing right there in the room, and she ripped the mask off his face, kicking him out. Just then, the doctor finally arrived, and within minutes, I gave birth. A little boy.

After they all left, I finally had a moment to bond with my son. He was perfect. But in the middle of the night, an old nurse came in to collect urine samples from both of us. She was harsh, and she made him cry. By the next day, I was told I could no longer be alone with my baby. CPS had taken custody, and I wouldn't be leaving the hospital with him.

I felt the shock, but at the same time, it wasn't surprising. Anxiety and depression washed over me. I begged to stay longer, to buy more time with my baby. He was so beautiful. The staff gave me two more days, but I knew time was running out. When I asked what would happen if I resisted, they said security would remove me, and if I caused any trouble, the police would arrest me. Back then, CPS wasn't focused on reuniting parents with their children—it was all so harsh. And in the end, it's always the children who suffer the most, never understanding why.

I spent two days with my son in the hospital. He never left my arms, and I smelled him all day and night long. A nurse had to be in my room 24/7 when he was with me. He had olive skin like me and his father. I was impressed with our genes. I knew it was Jesse's baby from the time he was in the work furlough. This little nugget was from him and heaven. I was going to have to leave him with strangers and he would never love me. Another epic failure. Depression, anger, and resentment kicked in. My baby was the victim.

The day came to be discharged. I was asked to leave him, and I didn't want to give him up. A friend called me and said that she was on her way to pick me up and to leave my baby. She said she would help me get him back. I said my goodbyes and my heart was once again ripped out of my body of my own cause and doing.

The Asian guy who was the trust fund son took pity and invited me to move into his place as he had other women there like me as well. It was his family home that he turned into the female meth shelter. He said I'd get along with them and they could support me through the process of losing my child. He promised he would help me for as long as he could. He was a nice guy. While I was not homeless at this point, I could no longer hold my baby and the future seemed grim. I carried that baby for nearly nine months, and to leave him as a newborn was beyond painful.

The CPS worker told me that I was entitled to one visit a month if she could schedule it with the foster parents. She further stated that I must be drug tested before encountering the baby. That was a challenge, as I was a full-blown meth head, deep into my addiction. But I cleaned up, gained weight, and I felt stable before the first visit. I entered the CPS building with anxiety, and I was so excited to meet him again as he was two months old then. He was irritable, crying, and making me feel like shit. There was no comfort from me—it actually annoyed me. I brought him a gift and he wasn't into me at all. I went dark and told myself that he didn't even love me. They did not have the next date in sight for me to visit with him. I was a fucking mess.

I was beyond depressed. I wanted to die. I went onto the next chapter of dark adventures by reconnecting with unsavory folks. I thought I was a worthless piece of shit, and the CPS worker had no desire to reunite me with my children. She abused me by yelling at me and telling me I would never be a good mother. No encouragement or assistance with the program that was once offered in the past where I could take my children back.

I fell back into that dark place—depressed, angry, and completely done with staying sober. All my kids were now wards of the state, and once again, I was nothing but an embarrassment to my family. I isolated myself, plunging headfirst into the drug world again. This time, I headed into the city without a care. I was unafraid to die, on a suicide mission, blunt and rude, with a newfound confidence. I'd had enough of being taken advantage of, and I was sick of having kids I couldn't seem to straighten out for.

I had no formal education. I dropped out of school, and the only positive figure in my life was my Russian dad, but even he had given up. He tried to adopt all three of my kids, but the courts wouldn't allow it, saying his heart condition made him unfit. So here I was, in the trenches, being used as a pawn in drug schemes. I was taken to gambling houses, stashing cash at my mom's house in the middle of the night, changing my hair color to stay under the radar. I bounced from one dangerous situation to the next, mixing Valium with meth to keep going. The combination numbed the depression, but it was a destructive path I couldn't seem to escape. Every day, I put myself in danger, hanging out with people who couldn't care less about me.

I was beaten, raped, and tortured by multiple men. One night, I found myself in the projects with some shady people who tried to steal the little I had. When I left, I ended up at a major freeway, wearing dark clothes. I lay down in the middle of a busy intersection, cars speeding past me. I wanted one of them to hit me. I was exhausted, both mentally and physically, and I just wanted it all to end. Lying there, I whispered to the sky, "Lord, take me away. I don't deserve to be here; I don't deserve to be a mother."

I must've passed out, because the next thing I remember was the sound of horns blaring. Five young Japanese guys in a Mercedes station wagon pulled over, thinking I was some discarded carpet. When they realized I was a person, they dragged me off the road and put me in their car. I was dazed and confused, but one of them was crying. When I asked why, he said, "Because of you."

It hit me then—I was traumatizing these innocent young men who probably had no idea what drugs or this kind of life even looked like. I felt worse than ever. I told them to let me go, that I'd figure it out on my own, but they refused. They drove me to their place—a small apartment attached to a garage. It turned out that they lived near my sister Jennifer, though I didn't realize it at the time. They offered me a shower, fresh clothes, and a place to rest. They were like guardian angels sent to save me when I'd lost all hope.

I was in shock as I washed my hair and changed into their clothes. They were high, but not too far gone—just dabbling in marijuana and meth. Despite everything, they treated me with kindness. I ate leftover beef curry, sat down, and for the first time in a long time, someone asked me if I was okay. I tried to brush it off, telling them I'd be fine, but they insisted I stay until I was stronger. I couldn't help but laugh. They had no idea the hell I'd been through. But I stayed, rested, and left two days later feeling like a different person. They prayed for me, wished me well, and never once treated me poorly or touched me inappropriately. These boys, my unexpected angels, saved my life.

As I left, I felt clean, like I could finally breathe again. I decided to call CPS, hoping I could turn things around for my kids. But when I reached out, the worker told me I was a lost cause and hung up on me. I went there but no one at the office would help me, and I was told I'd be arrested for harassment if I didn't leave. *WTF? Really, you are seriously the biggest cunt on earth!*

That's when I gave up again. I headed back to the city, determined to get high again, this time to make sure I wouldn't come back. I was ready to fly high and finally give that CPS worker what she wanted—my death.

I was walking into a hotel lobby to use the restroom and out of the corner of my eye, I saw a large guy who was a wise guy, but not a goodfella. They were the solid gangsters, the ones that should never be allowed to even call themselves a wise guy. They should be clipped, as most of the families did not tolerate bullshit within a crew. There is always a thorn in a rosebush, my sister Kate would tell me. And, in this case, we had potential black rose candidates. I saw him staring at me as if I was a lowlife, but I did not resemble one. Whenever I got arrested, they would take my mugshot and ask the attending officer who brought me in if it was valid that I was a drug addict. I had all my teeth, a nice complexion (as I took care of it with expensive creams—habit from my mom since age nine), a nice body, and I was sharp with the tongue, with the street intuition of a magician.

So, this obvious creeper was staring at me. I ignored him and headed to the restroom. I came out to use the pay phone and he came up next to me. I didn't make the actual call, as I just dialed a wrong number to see what he did next. He came next to me, dropped a quarter and said, "I apologize, please excuse me," as he was bending down to pick up the coin.

I looked at him and smiled, and that's it, he was Jell-O. I am not boasting or being conceited; he was ugly and near a young hot chick in tight jeans with a red top, a red shiny purse and red shiny sandals, with glossy Lip Life lipstick and heavy gloss. He told me that he and his buddies were upstairs in room 1609 and they had dope, martinis, and Valium. I laughed and asked, "You take me for a chronic?"

He said something to the effect of "Never," but he just wanted to offer some fun. I chuckled and told him I was game. I got in the elevator, and was on my way to hell again.

These guys were dealers as they had way too much dope to be functional users. The wise guys who used the dope were not decent. The true Don and made guys never touched the stuff. They may have had businesses that were involved in drug trades and related activities, but not typically. It was the unions and other ways they made money and laundered. The Cosa Nostra operated like any other businessman would. It was the Cugine (young soldiers striving to be made men) where they had the problems. This was especially true if the guy had a mental illness or what is now known as cognitive or behavioral issues. These guys were the bad Cugine and would never become made men. I guarantee it.

I did so much dope and took a couple Valium to calm down, but it wasn't working, so I smoked more meth, and could feel my heart beating in my chest. It was raging and my hearing became like the Bionic Woman. *It's a true trait on ice. Trust me. It was like I put hearing aids on, and I could hear exactly what the goofballs were saying in the bedroom of the suite I was in.*

They were huddled and planning a gang rape scenario. And small fucking world—one of them was from Mr. L's condo that day, watching the game. I knew I was about to get raped. I may have wanted to die, but raped? Fuck these clowns, I was out of there. My heart was nearly out of my chest, but I told them I forgot I had to meet my uncle downstairs and he's a goodfella. They backed off and let me leave as they were not sure which wise guy this was, and they already knew me, so they couldn't tell if it was legit, and they would get clipped in a dark alley. I left and ran down the street as fast as I could.

I came up to an Izakaya-type restaurant—a line of cooks behind a counter where they prepared fresh Gyoza, Ramen, Udon, Curry Bowls, and Musubi. It was called the Beef Stew Bowl. I entered, and the girl at the front with the blue apron said, "Irasshaimase," meaning welcome. I nodded to be polite, and she sat me at the bar/countertop. I ordered a beef curry bowl with white rice and pickled vegetables and a Sprite. I put my purse on the back of the tall stool and that was the last thing I remember, until I woke up on the street in front of the restaurant.

The EMT was asking me the same questions I'd been asked each time someone called the ambulance in the past for me. *What year is it? What day is it? Who is the President of the United States? What year were you born? What is your home address?* And, if one was unresponsive or answered any of those questions incorrectly, you're being wheeled and lifted into an ambulance with an IV of Diazepam (Valium). I guess I hit my head hard.

From what I was told, I put my purse on the back of the stool and went into a full-blown overdose seizure right in the restaurant. I flipped all over the tile floor like a fish and bled from chewing my tongue to near pieces. I foamed at the mouth, and I was dragged outside to the street, as the customers were freaking out. 911 was called and paramedics arrived. I was laying down when I saw a familiar face from the street. He walked over me as he was passing by. He and I connected eyes, and he made no attempt to help or render aide for fear of being connected to the incident, I suppose. He was from a good family as well.

The EMTs stabilized me and told me I had to go into the ambulance. I refused and said I had no medical insurance. They told me it wasn't about that, it was about my well-being.

One of them said, "What was described to us seems like there needs to be a physician to look at you."

I was wheeled into the ambulance, and they hooked me up with the IV drip and then I was calm, as the Valium was setting in and I no longer had my heart beating a million miles a minute. I was wheeled in on a gurney and left in a dimly lit hallway. The smell and fluorescent lights were unmistakable. Looking down, I saw my body ridden with red welts. I was temporarily distracted from the intense itch by the screeching sound of a toddler crying echoing down the corridor.

I ended up in the same ER they always took me to. I wish we had a choice. It was the best hospital in Queens, but it was embarrassing seeing the same doctors and nurses over and over again. Dr. Goto did not have the night off. *Fuck my life. OMG, he's gonna be pissed.* You see, we had become acquaintances in the sense that he saw me far too often on his table and he gave me the same speech each time. I wanted to run. He came into my room and said,

"Well, well, Marie, you are back to visit me. How nice of you to stop by. You shouldn't have."

I am like—*this motherfucker again! I get it!*

He then looked at the chart and said, "Oh, did you get your takeout since you missed your dinner at the Beef Stew Bowl?"

What a real dick, I mean, so real that I should have listened. He was an uncle's age to me. And he was not happy at all. I was ready for the lecture of the night.

He said, "By statistics and this trend of repeat instances, you will be dead in a year from one source or another."

I got up and told him, "Treat me or I am leaving."

He said, "Marie, you should go to the treatment center here. I promise to cut the line and claim you are a VIP referral from him."

Oy Vey! I graciously declined and took my prescription and left.

He yelled from the hallway as I walked down the hall with my finger up, "The next time is a toe tag to the morgue, Marie. Adios, Amiga!"

Word on the street was the guy who saw me blabbed to all the druggies, so everyone was scared I was going to OD on their watch or in their hotel room. I was being avoided by the drug dealers who normally loved having me around. I was on my own in terms of the hustle to live. I met up with a girl from my past who had her shit together, it seemed. She was a functioning addict and took pity on me as we were childhood friends who played Barbie together. Her sister dated my brother Peter, and she was now a born-again Christian. Her sister told her to take me in and help me get back on my feet. Putting us together ended up not being the best idea, truthfully. We were both toxic for each other. She was a mother of a ten-year-old and married to a dabbler. Her father was a full-blown meth head, and he drove a white van and took me around when I needed a ride. I slept under her son's top bunk and she and her husband were in the same large studio. I ended up moving into the garage, so I'd have my space and only had to come in for food and the bathroom. It was better. After all, she and I, plus her pops, would rage all night long and be up until the sun came up.

The ADHD kicked in and I was beginning to feel bored, as we were in a small apartment across the street from a hospital. She introduced me to a huge drug dealer, and I immediately didn't like him as he had the God complex and expected me to bow. He came over and gave us dope if she fucked him. *OMG, seriously?* I was so turned off by this gorilla of a clown. She did her trip, and I connected with a friend who had smaller amounts of meth, but he was cool and didn't make a pass at me. He just liked to hang out and listen to classic rock, and we walked with the Walkman through the streets and danced. It was fun and silly, but at least I wasn't being raped or being cornered by gang bangers. I was safe and in a decent home with my childhood friend. Her husband caught her giving Gorilla a blow job and she got the ultimatum, and to boot, he said that I had ten days to move out, as I was causing her to do acts that were not becoming of a wife. *Wait a minute. What? She was doing this before I stayed at her house. Well, I had to be the fall girl and leave.*

I was at the Walkman guy's house and he asked if I could grab dope, and I said I could from a nasty gorilla in Queens. He gave me the money and said if I didn't come back, he'd get his boxer girlfriend to kick my ass. I agreed and paged the gorilla. He answered right away, and we met at a yellow apartment that looked abandoned. *Terrific, now what do I do?* Well, I went inside, of course, as I had to deliver Mr. Walkman's dope, or I'd get my ass kicked by his psycho pro boxer of a girlfriend. She was gnarly and she could scrap, and I was tired of the black eyes and vertigo.

The gorilla escorted me in the house and there was a huge recliner there facing the door. There was a candle he lit and another camping lamp that ran on batteries. There was running water but no electricity. It was hot in there, so he opened the window. There was a small end table with an ashtray and a torch lighter, like for Crème Brulee. He took a large baggie, filled up the pipe, and handed it to me with the torch. I lit it and took a massive hit. I felt the euphoria like Jesse did when he blew out a hit of the blue rock. I was spinning and in the clouds. He turned to me and said, "You seem like you'd be a good dealer."

I thought—*Why me?* He further stated that I had all the qualities of a smart businesswoman and that if I was trained properly, I could morph into dealership. I was thinking—*Is this guy serious?* I nodded, grabbed the pipe, and hit it again. He then told me that I couldn't smoke too much, or I wouldn't make money. I had to control the habit and then I would be good and able to balance it all.

Okay, am I buying dope or did I walk into this shithole of an apartment for dealer training? Get the fuck outta here, you clown.

He then said, "I'll give you an ounce to start, but you have to give me a hand job."

OMG, what the fuck. He pulled out the large baggie and I was pondering. He told me I could make thousands off that bag alone and he would sponsor me, and as long as I gave him the hand job, I could keep the dope. I looked at him. He was disgusting—big and looming over me. I had to decide. I grabbed the dope and did the deed. *How fucking horrible!* He had a small, pathetic dick. *Whatever I wanted to tell myself to make me feel better.*

I left with an ounce of meth, and I felt like barfing, which I did down the street. And then I said to myself—*Marie, it's a new start.*

You will never do that again by force or pressure. It happened once and now you have your own shit.

I disciplined myself and I made money. My first regular customer was Mr. Walkman, who bought dope three times a week. I did the math on quadrupling that amount and there I was, a new narco on the street. I was no longer part of the lowlife homeless people. I was now able to afford vacation rentals, and I moved around town and slept at my girlfriend's house in the city (she was one of my customers, as well). She let me use her car and then I rented a convertible for a month. I was on cloud nine.

I kept building my small business. It was growing and I had fans and solid working customers. My favorite was the guy from the docks. He was married with kids. He worked the graveyard shift with the Matson containers on the crane, and he needed to stay up, so he faithfully bought a baggie each night of work to discipline himself and not smoke it in one night. He paid top dollar and always tipped. I loved it—gratuity! *Wow, who would have known.*

The boys in the industry heard about me, including a new guy! He and I were on the same frequency. He loved the Bee Gees and Donna Summer. Enough said. We were partnering up and both making money. He was a trust fund baby and had to take care of his grandfather as part of the deal. He was Japanese and I understood the culture well. He was helping me and then one day, I slept over at his house. He didn't try anything on me as I had my own bed in the corner that he designated. But when I woke up, I saw blood on the pillow that I was sleeping on. I looked over and he was on the phone and told whomever he was talking to that he had to go. He hung up and looked at me with this weird, concerned look. He shook his head and said, "You had a seizure, and you were chewing your tongue. You should lay off the shit and just sell it."

I was shocked, as this was not the first time I was being told that after coming out of an attack. I acknowledged it and then I sat up. He told me it was scary at first, but he realized it was similar to an epileptic seizure, and maybe I had a form of epilepsy. I called the urgent care, and was prescribed Dilantin—an anti-seizure drug. I now had prevention care. *OMG, what a way to abuse the meds.*

It was a drought, as they called it, when the narcs would seize the big dealers in the city and surrounding areas. It was difficult to find good dope and the ones who had it hid it, as they would take the risk of being robbed or killed if they knew who had the crypt, as we used to say then. More like *Tales from the Crypt*. I was at a hotel room my friend had offered for me to stay at, shower, and use for the rest of the week. I took him up on it and was a bit down, as was my dope and my pocketbook.

I called a guy who was a scumbag of the earth. He told me that he had the good shit. He came over, gave me dope, and we argued. Before I knew what was happening, he was raping me. I was so disgusted and crying, experiencing PTSD, and not realizing it. I called my girlfriend and she said she would pick me up and take me somewhere to rest and chill. She picked me up in a red Thunderbird with a Mexican guy I didn't know and another friend in the front seat.

I was in the back right side by the small window of that '90s T-Bird. She was on the left next to me. I proceeded to tell her what happened, and the next thing I knew, I woke up on the grass in front of BB's house, and he was looking down at me from above the wall. I had saliva all around my mouth and I was in excruciating pain in my left shoulder. It felt like it was not connected to the rest of my body. I squirmed and BB said, "You should rest it as it's dislocated. I can tell." He shook his head and lit up a Benson & Hedges cigarette. Another reason I liked him—we smoked the same type of cigarettes.

The story that I was told by my friend was horrific. I was in the back seat explaining that I got raped by the creeper and she turned and said I looked like Linda Blair in *The Exorcist*, apparently. I had a grand mal seizure this time. She panicked, and her friend who was driving was flipping and racing to BB's house, so they could put me there until I came out of it. That dumbass friend of mine tried to hold me down and fight with me to keep me from throwing myself against the window and back seat. He nearly had a panic attack. I tore my own shoulder out of its socket. Yes, my neighbors today think I got into a waterskiing accident, but that is the story instead of all this. Who would ever imagine or understand this?

I heard the sirens approaching and asked BB to turn it off. He told me, "You want it off as bad as I do."

His grandpa came out of his cottage and BB told him to go back inside. He shook his head and went back inside. I was now being cornered by EMTs and they were once again asking me the same fucking questions. *What is the date today? What is the president's name? What is your home address?* I didn't know any of it as I was wiped out. They were worried and set up the IV. I was being hooked up to liquid Diazepam and I felt like my head was going back into another seizure. The EMT grabbed my head and turned me to the side and the Valium started kicking in. I was calm and realizing I had an attack. I was so embarrassed. The Mexican was walking back and forth. He didn't look good, and he left and said that he was never smoking meth again. He was traumatized. I was glad I scared him away.

BB was disappointed in me. Not only did I bring unwelcome attention to his house, but I didn't listen to his advice. Also, I had a seizure when I was sexually abused. That was a connection for sure as this always happened after an attack on me. He never made a pass at me and told me to get off the death wish as it was unbecoming and a turnoff as a friend. We hung out a couple more times thereafter, but he was about to turn himself in for a long sentence and he said he was cleaning up his life. He said I inspired him!

That day, I was taken back to my friend, Dr. Goto, and I didn't wait long as he came in stomping this time. I was on the gurney, and I stared into the stainless steel table with wheels so I could avoid eye contact with him. He entered and said, "Sit up, Marie, so I can put your shoulder back in place, and then we are having a talk."

I was thinking—*here we fucking go. Spare me, as I am not listening to you, Doc. I have a hard head and a death wish. I am a shitty parent, and I want to die. I am worthless and don't want to live anymore.*

He turned to me, and I was standing up looking at him. He said to stare into his eyes and just keep still, no matter what. He slammed my shoulder back into place and I barfed on the floor from the pain. *OMG, are you kidding me? Holy shit, Doc, you are strong and obviously pissed.* He told me that I needed to see an orthopedic surgeon and fix it quickly as I injured it badly. I asked how long his fix would last and he said, "You're lucky if you get five years and it'll come out all the time and be debilitating."

He came with up to my face and said, "Marie, you will be with a toe tag on your foot, and I won't be the attending physician. Get clean and take care of yourself. I don't know how you're still alive."

I left and waited for my dad at the front. Instead, he sent my brother Brad in, and I was shocked. Brad shook his head and said, "The shit must've been good." He handed me $100 cash, got in his car and said, "Take care of yourself." He drove away in his Toyota 4Runner. I was there alone, and I looked down and felt 120%

pathetic right about now. My tongue hurt like a motherfucker from being chewed on to near death. I shook my head and decided Mr. B was the safest place to be right now. *OMG, really? Did I not learn then?*

I was once again the butler to Mr. B. I was opening the front door, making people wait in the living room, cooking, cleaning, and taking small hits here and there as no one wanted to give me dope. I had money stashed at Mom's still and I realized I had a tiny fortune. It was time to get cracking with the deals so I could rent an apartment and get my shit together, and hopefully my sister-in-law would sneak the kids over so I could see them (the older two, that is). My third child, who I had to leave at the hospital, had now been adopted by a famous athletic family, as my sister Jennifer traded the baby for cheap rent in one of their cottages. The deal with her and them was that I was never allowed near my son, nor could I make any attempt to contact him.

I was back deep into the world of the dope dealers and seeing large amounts of cocaine and meth. I was doing my best to not get high as much. I reignited my clientele, and I was being warned against my practice and being told it was a small town with jealous people. I didn't listen and I was living in the city from hotel to hotel and apartment to apartment again. I was in the city with a chick that was a small dealer, and we were delivering something to her friend. We were walking on the street and a guy looked so familiar. He looked at me, and lo and behold, it was Brad, my older brother. Gee, the last time I saw him, he was doing well and left me at the hospital. Tonight, he seemed tweaked out, and he was. We caught up, and I brought him back to my hotel room. I gave him dope and fell asleep. He left his number of his friend's house and said that he would meet me the next night. I was puzzled and so happy I ran into him! *We are kindred spirits, and now he's getting high, so he's one of us. Cool beans.*

CHAPTER 12: THE GOOD BROTHER AND SWAT TEAM SALLY

After I barely recognized my own brother walking down the street in the city, we ended up hanging out daily. He told me he was living at his friend's house and had split up with his wife. I asked why and he told me he caught her giving a guy head in a park near their house. *Wow, she couldn't go to another town?* It was meant to be because he saw her true colors. She accused him of beating her and had him removed by the cops and filed a TRO, so she could bring her boyfriend home to fuck him in their bed. I got the impression that Brad was depressed over her, and especially since she was keeping the kids from him. He was a great father and husband. He provided well. He had real estate and worked for the motion pictures as a greens guy (setting up the plants on set). He was in both unions and got paid well.

We were hanging out on the daily, thick as thieves and getting high together. He wanted to meet a cute friend of mine, and I told him to take a break as he just separated from his wife. But I ended up introducing him to one of my friends. He developed an immediate crush. She wasn't even that cute, but she had a personality and was also a small dope dealer. That last part was a non-negotiable if you were a long-term user. There was no other way to afford it.

He wanted to meet Mr. B and they got acquainted and started doing large deals that even I was afraid of. He dealt to a tranny with the dog in the walk-up apartment in Queens who loved him as a friend. She was cool. He ended up moving in with my friend and I was against it, but whatever, he was a big boy. They started to get serious and were settling down. He didn't allow me to get dropped off at his house and I had to meet him at a gas station or cemetery. Then he would pick me up and drive me in or I had to walk down the street alone and ensure no one followed me. Why? We were deep in the realm of dope, deals, and money. That's why. I was feeling pretty good and having fun, hanging out with B and Brad, who said the heat was after him. I was in denial, which is not a river in Egypt. But I ignored his concerns.

Brad and I were both tired of being vagrants and living from condo to hotel to a vacation rental to a friend's house, and then just being these strangers in the night. We longed for stability as druggies—*how funny is that?* We were tired of packing up and moving every week or even less at times, depending on how much shit we had in our possession, how much we used, and the company we were keeping. He and I were both dealing to make ends meet. I decided I wanted to settle down like him, but I was not as secretive. I was an idiot who got sloppy and was asking to get caught. *No glory in it, as the shit was literally rotting our bodies, inclusive of bones and teeth, right out of our skulls.*

I was staying in this weird old hotel in a part of town that was lower end, where we fit in and were able to do our trip in the room and neighborhood. We had friends in other buildings nearby that the group of us commingled with, and we would travel back and forth to and from each unit. This was what I called intentional homelessness. Gypsy shit classic. We frequented a house outside the city that was clean and nice, with a divorcee who was on a drug war path, as he was bitter. He was left in that house and he bought and sold petty dope as well. My inner circle consisted of B, Brad, Brad's girlfriend, another girl who hung around B, the divorcee, and a cousin who played the "I am innocent" role but would do more dope than we did. I had another group of Asians that were close to me, and they were very careful. One was a Chinese dude who purposely had an untidy house, so it wouldn't attract the chronics. The other guy was known as Speed—he had the good fucking dope. He and his wife adored me, and we were close. I would stay over at their house, eat, and play Lawnmower Man on the Atari with Speed. He was funny and had a funky eye from a fight gone bad. He had leather jackets that girls would pawn and other jewelry. He was very cool and respectful. Asians didn't rape or make passes. They were raised well. Completely platonic, which was so nice.

The Chinese guy sold me a car, an old Valiant from the '60s. Another druggie Asian guy idiot outsmarted me and stole it, then sold it in the projects. I loved that car—made of real steel. There were so many people who took advantage of my kindness for weakness. And, when I would fall asleep, they would pull the Kadafi on me. I had one girl that was my friend-"ish" and she felt bad for robbing me, so she left me her Gio Armani perfume bottle in my lap with a note telling me that she robbed me. Her boyfriend made her do it, she claimed. So, because of this shit, I got sick of the BS as it happened too many times and I was being stalked by people, as they knew I had to sleep at some point. I would pay my friend to watch me and she would get high and do that. She locked us in with the deadbolt and let me shower there and keep a bag. There were also two guys that were transvestites and performers at the gay club. They fed me and bought dope. I had so much fun with them and one was a badass seamstress. I never learned how to sew and had no desire. She could sew dresses and costumes for the shows they were in.

One night, Brad called me through the pager, and I called him back from a pay phone that was a vetted one that he would instruct me to use in the city. He was so fucking paranoid and careful—something I lacked at that point. He was friends with all kinds of cops from working on the movie sets and being in the union IATSE and Teamsters along with my brother Peter and my father. We all hung out at the movie set. My brother Peter sold coke to all the stars and crew on set, and got everyone hooked on the blue Peruvian flake. *Boy, it was awful.*

Brad was so strung out on a movie set and couldn't stand the director, so he picked him up off the ground and choked him nearly to death. He wasn't a violent person—at least to me—but I had heard stories from his ex-girlfriends years later and they said that he was one of those guys that went crazy. I guess I could see that. But now that he was in my life and I was in his again, he felt protective. He asked me to meet him in a nightclub in Jersey toward the back, order a drink, act like I was cruising there and wanting to dance, and play the part. I was like, "Really?"

He said, "You better listen and just meet me there."

So, I got there and followed his directions. He showed up all incognito in black and acted like he ran into me there by coincidence. I was like—*Come on, bro! You must be smoking the good shit.*

He told me, "My friend, the undercover, said you need to stop hanging out with B."

He further stated that I was going to be part of the bust, as they were following him daily and knew I was a close friend for years and part of the entourage. He gave me the big brother warning, as the narc told him to tell me to stay away no matter what, and to lay low for a long time to let the heat die down. *Do you think I listened? Of course not!* I kept being a part of B's group and helping him do deals so I could pay for the rent and save up for an apartment in Brooklyn. I wanted out of the city and the normal places I hung out. Everyone made fun of me and said I was nuts.

I lived on the outskirts of the city and found a place with the divorcee. He rented me a room at the back of his house and said the hallway bathroom was mine, and he had his master bedroom. He had another room in the back that was a spare, as it was his kids' old room, who no longer came to the house, for obvious reasons. I had use of the kitchen and I could park on the street. I loved that town, as it was close to stores, restaurants (not like we ate out that much), parks, a school, and other close conveniences where B would often stop by. I became stable and a friend rented a car for me long-term. I was independent, driving, and living on my own—what I always wanted for myself—not to be reliant on an abusive man. I was proud of myself even though I was completely out of my mind and not thinking about consequences or reality.

I had given up on my kids, as CPS would not help me, and I couldn't stay sober longer than three days by that point. And that was usually when I was sleeping. I was "*living on the edge*" like the Aerosmith song. *Totally. WOLO, YOLO,* and I didn't care if I died as I had failed epically as a parent. I chose to be a wannabe entrepreneur slinging deals so that I could have a stable place, help others, and get caught because I didn't listen to Brad. Remember the movie, *Less than Zero*? That'd be me.

Brad became distant and stopped coming over. He was afraid of losing his freedom, as I was so careless. I had a guy from the neighborhood who was my brother's and sister's classmate from high school. He came over to smoke dope and visit me at this house. He was an educated Italian guy who loved to eat Italian food, smoke dope, get paranoid, and then run home to his parents' house in the hood, as he knew he was safe there. He brought over Puttanesca, my favorite dish from the little place on the corner. And one night, he told me, "You need to build a trap door to the underneath of the house that has a tunnel into the ground that can't be sniffed out by dogs."

"Are you fucking serious? What do you think this is? I am small time."

Well, I guess kilos in my eyes were not as much as it's not quite equivalent to pounds, but that was the level of elite I was swimming in. He told me that I should do it immediately, as he had weird vibes around the house I was in and swore he saw people hiding in the bushes or in the dumpsters out on the street, and he felt the hair on his neck stand up. He was spiritual and in tune with the vibration for sure. *Did I listen? Nope. I pushed it off.* I thought they were all fucking paranoid from doing too many drugs.

I met a guy through my cousin, and his friend owned a huge garage that fixed cars and offered mechanical (and other) services. They wanted to buy coke. I was like, "I don't sell it, but I know someone who does in those amounts."

I made the deal happen, as it would have meant two months of rent this time around for my cut. Oh boy, at that time, rent was $700-$800 a month near the city. I went through with researching and helping that guy with the request, as the "facilitator." (It's ironic to me that today I am still a facilitator, but in healthy ways.) The landlines were dangerous, and I was getting sloppy at this point, discussing sensitive data over the phone. I was too lazy to do the trip that Brad said to always do. Use the pager, go to the pay phone, change it up, and don't ever call right back. *Did I listen? No.* I got too comfortable and would be waking up from a two-day bender, so who would want to use the pager, go to the pay phone, and be safe? Not me. Yes, it was illegal to tap a phone; however, not if they had suspicion and a judge awarded it. Apparently, they wanted B so badly and I was with or near him, so I was just as much of an interest. At the time, I didn't think or listen. I was in that river of denial in Egypt again.

I was hanging out with a brother of the guy who raped me in the hotel before the grand mal. If you're thinking, *Horrible choices,* yes, you would be totally right. *Oh Vey.* I was up to my neck at this point, not listening to any warning signs. I was in bliss with a guy that just wanted me for my dope—the shoe was officially on the other foot. I thought he was nice as he had a job and a place to live (high standards, what can I say), but he was still in love with the ex (who wasn't really an ex). Between that guy, not paying attention to what my friend said about the trap door, and others telling me about the vibes outside and so forth, I just kept on going. The phones were used to set up the deal and I allowed B and his flavor of the month, who was his steady side salad, to come over. She was nice, but just wanted to get high and stoned all day long and not work. She did whatever he wanted and watched him. She had only half her teeth. She had a way to smile to conceal it though. *Good for her.* The guy who was using me said he heard something in the roll off outside and asked who was doing construction, as no one had any active projects on the street. *Did I listen and send someone to check the dumpster? Nope.*

The other guys arrived at the house, and they all went into my bedroom. B was in the other room prepping the dope. I was getting high in the hallway. The money was exchanged, and I was talking with the user guy who didn't really like me for me. There was the girl with the half grill (teeth) and B's daughter, age seven. *Why in the fuck would anyone bring a child into this situation?* I was about to go into the bathroom when I heard loud banging. I didn't understand what it was, but I saw images outside the jalousie windows that were not clear to look inside. I saw the front door shaking and I was now realizing it was a forced entry. I grabbed whatever dope I saw laying around and flushed it down the toilet. I heard guys outside yelling, "She flushed it! Take the door down!"

I peeked outside, and Boom! The front door was knocked down by a battering ram. I couldn't believe what I was seeing. I ran into the bathroom and screamed, laying on the floor, with my hands up. A red-headed officer entered with a plexiglass shield, a helmet, a handgun, and a rod. I was nearly pissing in my pants. He told me to keep my hands up and stay down.

"Stay down, so no one gets hurt!" he screamed.

I was fading into darkness and all I could hear were Brad's warnings over and over again.

I saw my entire life of only twenty-six years flash in front of my eyes in a split second. I was beyond remorseful, and I felt like I was going to have a heart attack from the crazy amount of anxiety I was feeling. We were in a full-blown drug bust. The cops had knocked down the solid 36" front door with an apparatus that knocked it off the hinges. I heard glass breaking and more screaming, plus the "Oh shits" coming from my room. I ignored it as I thought I was really going to be shot by the red-haired burly narc detaining me in the bathroom.

"Keep your hands up!"

I got pulled off the ground and tossed onto the couch next to the others. Our hands were zip-tied behind our backs and to each other. The house was being torn upside down. The K9 unit came in, the helicopters were flying above, the neighbors—quiet Japanese people—were standing outside like the fucking Stones came to town. We were pale as ghosts—quiet and fucked. I had no idea zip ties immobilize you, but they sure do!

The Amway laundry soap was being dumped out and they were calling out the items and putting them in the evidence locker from one of the investigators. This went on for hours. I was mouthing off, as usual. "Leave my fucking Amway alone!" I screamed.

The narc by me said, "The Amway is the fucking least of your problems, girl."

I was hysterical—I was busted and never going to get my kids, let alone be an independent woman away from the abusive boyfriends where I felt codependent. I was losing my freedom as each minute ticked by. I was lost, remorseful, bummed, disappointed—a million feelings all at once were clouding my heart and soul, yet I was fully aware of all the actions, vibrations, senses, and humans in the room. My mind was racing.

One of the agents asked me, "Are you a new chronic?"

I replied, "What the fuck?"

He told me that I had looked young, not as weathered as the rest of the group or seasoned by the meth. He could tell I was naïve in so many ways, and of course, the only emotional one with remorse out of the group. I was clearly like the Sesame Street song lyrics, "One of these things is not like the others; one of these things doesn't belong." And yes, I did feel that way inside. I was so ashamed of myself, of what I had become, and the fact that I made such poor choices that I was going to be on the 10:00 news with my unsavory co-defendants.

This was also the night before Thanksgiving when everyone back then was home prepping for the big holiday. In New York City, the huge culinary community, is where I made my debut of fuckery on Thanksgiving Eve 1996. Relatives and many acquaintances saw the clip and then it ran again the next day, and my mother found out as my aunt called her to break the news. I was now public news. *Good grief. And Happy Thanksgiving to my family!*

About a month earlier, a group of us went out on a walk during the dusk hour and decided to go to the Safeway to buy ice cream and stretch our meth legs and lungs. It was at that time that I had a friend with us, who showed me the narcs hiding in the nearby roll offs and the neighbor's fences down the street. Once again, I felt this person was feeling paranoid and maybe up for too long. He was not wrong; he really did see all of that and he didn't get busted with us. Good for him!

It was now hours after the raid entry. The narcs finally threw us in patrol cars, and they put me and half-grill girl in one car. B was alone and the other guys together in another patrol car. We were taken to the local police station in town and booked, fingerprinted, and my photo was taken. They pushed me into a cold cell with a huge echo. The cell had brick walls, a plastic mattress with no sheet or blanket, a soft fun house mirror I could poke with my finger to make a dent and pop back out, cement floors that were freezing cold, a stainless steel toilet with no seat cover, and a sink that looked like it was a box with a faucet that barely ran any water. I was dressed in black high-top hikers, a pair of Calvins, and an oversized Ralph Lauren sweatshirt for comfort, as the cop who said I didn't match with the rest of the crew suggested I wear something warm since I'd be spending the entire holiday weekend in the hoosegow. I would never see that house again.

I don't know what my mug shot looks like, and thank God it wasn't available online back then. I was in the cell on the night before Thanksgiving. That was Wednesday. I realized I was not going to eat a nice meal the next night. *Really? Like I deserved it!* So, I stayed in there and the cell block guys came around to feed me by sliding a tray through the door. The food was awful, and I mean absolutely fucking terrible! This was all connected to the sting operation, where crooked cops were taking the funds to buy prisoners the shitty food and were buying Costco steak and lobster for themselves. The pigs in the zoo ate better than us in there.

But I knew I didn't have a lot of room to complain. It was now Black Friday, and I was not having a good time and shopping at Macy's. I was coming down off ice and I was remorseful, depressed, and turned into a lunatic. I screamed, shouted, and demanded to get out of there. I stomped my feet against the cement floors. No one responded. No one cared. Then, on Saturday, I was so down and in a very dark spot. A narc came in and said that I needed to follow him. He knew I was desperate and weak. He and another detective pulled me into an interrogation room, and I was now being questioned by these two cops.

They were pressuring me and said, "Tell us the truth and we may let you go."

I requested an attorney, and they said no one knew I was there, and I couldn't get one as it was Thanksgiving weekend. They wanted me to rat on B. But I refused. I was so tired, and I never told on anyone except myself. So stupid, yet this was my way of coming clean. The cops asked me and tried to coerce me down a path. I said, "Nope, it wasn't like that. I needed rent and I brought people together."

They told me that I was going to take the hit as the shit was tossed into a bag under the bed in the room I rented and there just so happened to be a planner of mine with all my personal identifiers and the drugs went in there, allegedly. *Seriously, a Franklin Covey binder took me down? Who would have known?* At the end of the day, they asked me specifics and I said I didn't know what was happening. I let them conduct their personal affairs and to my knowledge, it was just a conversation, no dope deal. I gave them two bogus names of individuals and they wrote them down. I believe they vetted that, as they threw me in a new cell and said I would have my bail lowered—not released, but I was not in as much trouble.

Well, I totally made it worse, as I had implicated myself in the crime like an idiot and I didn't need to. I could have just said, "Wrong place, wrong time" like in the past. But, this time, it was like I was trying to prove that I was becoming stable in an inappropriate way to eventually get my kids back. Like I was really going to get them back while being in so deep with a kingpin drug dealer. *What a mess! Honestly!*

I was in the new cell, and it was Saturday night. I hadn't showered, as I couldn't get the fucking bird bath sink to turn on. I was awoken and unsure what time it was, as they were tiring me out. They said to me, "You now have a new bail amount and it's $200,000."

They threw papers at me in the cell, and I just flipped out and screamed "Fuck you!" and threw them in the air. They weren't supposed to do that to me! I was crying, as I had made my co-defendants appear more innocent than I was. I was now the target in the cell block.

On Sunday night, I was again beside myself. I still hadn't showered since Wednesday before the raid. It was days and nights later and I was losing my mind. My ADHD and withdrawals were getting the best of me. I prayed to God that I was forgiven and that I had made a huge mistake yet again in my life and for Him to take pity on me. *Really, Marie?*

I wished and hoped for the best as my court day was on Monday. The Paddy Wagon, as my mother called it, came to pick up the prisoners from the cell block. I was in the back of the vehicle with none of my co-conspirators. They kept us separated yet again and not even the girl with the half grill was there. I spotted a familiar face in the wagon, and it was one of the girlfriends of the Chinese guy with the intentionally dirty house. She was shocked that I was in there—they all heard the news. I told her I was going down for a long time. She told me to stay strong and she would give my message to the Chinese unclean guy that I was headed to jail. I didn't rat. I was taken to District Court for my arraignment. I stood before a judge who basically threw the pre-trial book at me and sentenced me to immediate jail time at Rikers Island. I was confused as I didn't realize they housed females there. Well, they did, in Module 3, to be precise.

I was now being transported to jail. It was actually a prison and classified as such (or I guess I should I say—correctional facility). This would be my new home for a bit. I was shaking in my boots, literally. I was processed and told I had to shower with the lice-medicated shampoo all over my body. I was given a towel, a nightgown-type uniform, and then a regular secondary uniform with an undershirt that was white. I was beside myself and they told me I was not able to wear my street clothes. They were to be kept at the front office and I would get them back when I was released (if I was released). It was like how prison is portrayed in movies, for sure. This was the real deal with serious criminals that ranged from murderers to rapists, to bank robbers and to us drug addicts.

Once I showered and was dressed in my new dark green army uniform, I was being referred to as "Marinelli"—my ex-husband's last name. It got me some respect though, as there were guards and inmates who knew of Rathe Marinelli. They did a cavity search on me and made me squat and cough. *And yes, it is as awful as it sounds!* The one guard told me that I needed to stay with a roommate and that I needed to stop showing my weakness and crying for being there. I didn't give a shit. I was emotional and this was tough to process. It was all hitting me like a ton of bricks that this time, I fucked up so badly that I was now locked up against my will with prison guards and multiple layers of walls, fencing, and barbed wire with scary motherfucking people.

Marie, you have to pay to play.

I was sobering up, or maybe I should say thawing out, from the meth/ice and I was clearly an unsavory individual who was now facing 27+ years from the huge mistake of being the "facilitator." The Commanding Officer (CO), Debbie, who was skinny, Portuguese, and pretty (at least for a guard), took one look at me and said to the rest of them, "Put Marinelli with Mishnaf."

Okay, that sounded French or Russian or Ukrainian, somewhat nice and mellow. I turned, and the bigger guard grabbed my arm while I held my towels and another uniform underneath it. I was clueless, and there was a blonde girl inside the room I was directed to. It was Miss Mishnaf, herself—a lady who seemed to be around eight years my senior. She had red lipstick on with thinner eyebrows from the '70s and she hugged me like she was my cousin from the Bronx, and we hadn't seen each other since we were kids or something. *Get the fuck outta here!* I chuckled an uncomfortable and half tearful smile as I was shaking and scared. *Boo Hoo, Marie, don't do drugs and hang out with murderers* is what was running through my mind. She closed the door and said, "Calm down. You are fine in my room and in this module. The worst person isn't even scary anymore. It's jail and it sucks, but you're not going to die in here with me or out there with those stupid bitches."

She opened a desk drawer and pulled out a cigarette and asked, "Do you smoke or what?"

I was like—*Does a bear shit in the woods? Of course I smoke.* She handed me a piece of chocolate first and said, "Priorities, girl."

"You can have chocolate in here?"

She said, "Yes, and I also have shampoo and conditioner, body wash, cocoa, a cup of noodles, and new pink lipstick."

I was thinking to myself—*Lord, you are watching over me, as how the hell did I end up in a room with Mishnaf?* I loved this chick to death right off the bat. She gave me the total rundown of all the other girls and said, "Keep to yourself, be neutral, and read in your room. The TV isn't worth being near girls that vibe you out and you'll never watch what you want, so do your own trip and get smart and read books."

She continued the lay of the land. "The puzzle table is off limits and the lady who sits at it, Jeanine, was an old bank robber getaway driver who has been in here for a long time. Leave her alone unless she talks to you."

"Okay, you got it. Thanks!"

She said, "I have to introduce you to Sally, the CNA, and a cool Filipino to us, but you must kiss her ass and be real at the same time."

So, I went outside and met Sally. She was a Filipino lesbian, with nice teeth, short black hair, clean, and was sitting at a desk with a phone near her. She had all the tools you need to clip your nails and toenails, Q-tips, scissors, Band-Aids, etc. She controlled the phone for calls that could be made at the station, or she'd let you use a private room for an attorney or sometimes your phone time, depending on who else was around. She took one look at me and said, "How the fuck did you get in here? You don't match the typical demographic."

I just looked at her, and she said, "You fucked up bad, huh?"

I said, "I am facing a lot of time for being in the wrong place at the wrong time."

She replied, "Wrong? You mean right," and she chuckled.

Mishnaf said, "She has a cigarette, and I am luckily included in the next smoke break." This was one of the best times to be in jail, I suppose, when cigarettes were allowed, but we had to walk outside and stand in a line, in an enclosed hallway outside of the module, while the guard with a gun watched us intently and then shuffled us back in once we were done with one cigarette. Sometimes, you would get lucky, and they would allow two in one break and a longer time, but that was pretty unusual.

I cried myself to sleep, of course, even though I knew I was safe … to a degree. I was in denial and not wanting to be there, but I fucked up so badly that they were throwing away the key. I had no hope at that point. I spent the next week trying to call anyone I could on the street to bail me out. But no one wanted anything to do with me. It was like I was a stranger, and no one cared that I was in there. I had no money or dope to pass out, and they were moving on to the next person as far as a friend or connection went. Some of them thought I ratted out others, but I did that to myself. I literally implicated myself at the center of the crime, and so, of course, I looked even more stupid to the drug addicts on the outside. My own brother was distancing himself from me, as he was paranoid that he was next. I didn't blame him. I would have felt the same way, if the shoe was on the other foot.

Since it was the holidays, a song contest was happening between modules. The grand prize was pizza from Pizza Hut to feed the entire module. I asked if there were any professional singers in the other units and the guards were like, "What kind of question is that?"

I said, "I want to know the odds and the chances we have in this group of females."

So, one of the guards told me that a great singer was down the hall.

I said, "What the fuck? We're never going to win, and we should all just give him the pizza and call it a day."

The guards laughed and the rest of the unit was like—*she's right!* The pretty guard made the announcement that it's not about the pizza, it's about caroling for the holidays. I said to myself—*Are you kidding me? We're in jail. Of course it's about the pizza! Just call it a day and let me sleep in misery and wake me up when it's New Year's Eve!* Well, our song was "Winter Wonderland." We practiced daily for weeks. *Guess who won the contest and ate the fucking pizza? Good old so and so. Get the fuck outta here. Moving on.*

At 8:57 p.m., the guard would yell, "Hot water and ice! Come get your hot water and ice before it's too late."

And we would line up like cattle and say, "Yay! It's hot water and ice time."

What was this for? Well, if you had money from working for $.25 or $.63 an hour, or a rich family member or boyfriend who put money in your account, then you had soda, cups of noodles, hot cocoa, and instant coffee with powdered creamer and sugar for your midnight snack before bed. You were allowed to get both hot water and ice, but only whatever you could carry of only one of each due to it being two types of temps and a mess to hold all the way back to your cell. I used it for cups of noodles and soda, but cocoa was nice before bed. At the end of the day, it was crap and made us fat. But seriously, what else did we have going for us?

I got a job folding laundry and was paid $.25 an hour. I asked if we had to stay at that rate or if there were raises or opportunities available with higher pay. The guard once again was like—*Who is this chick, hustling when she just arrived? Who the fuck does she think she is, the Queen of Rikers?*

What can I say, twenty-five cents seemed miniscule, and how the fuck was I going to buy the good conditioner (Finesse) and the better cocoa and cups of noodles? So, I kept asking guards and finally, a girl who was released opened up a kitchen position. That was $.63 an hour—a big raise! I was like, yes girl, I am there and getting in before anyone else. I am a chef, I belong there! So, I got the position, and I was told I must clean and not deal with the food. I said, "But I am a cook by heart, and I do well with food. Why would I want to waste my skills on cleaning? I don't mind it, really, but can I please touch the food?"

The girls were like—*Fuck off, you stupid loudmouth bitch.* So, of course there was a scuffle, and I had issues with one of the girls. The bank robber lady called me over to her table while she was playing puzzles one day. She told me to sit down because she wanted to talk to me.

I said, "About what?"

I was kind of afraid, but curious as to what she had to say.

She said, "Your mouth is going to cause issues for you in life wherever you go if you don't learn to grow up and control it. You have a chip on your shoulder and in jail, you should behave and start off humble when you arrive. If you keep going, you are going to run into problems."

She continued that she liked my spirit and motivation, but she said others wouldn't put up with it. So, I took her advice and started to look at myself. She was right. That fell right in line with my call that happened with my father. I called my dad, who was working on a motion picture in the city. He told me he was working to make extra hours and would bail me out when he was off the movie, which would be in a few months. I screamed and demanded he bail me out right at that moment.

He told it to me straight for the first time in my life up to that point. He said, "Marie, you made a huge mistake, and you are yelling at me like it's my fault? You have a rude awakening coming, honey. That chip on your shoulder has done you in this time, and I am not going to be the one to bail you out. When you calm down and lose that attitude, then I'll pick up your calls or call you. I must get back on set."

He hung up and I was dumbfounded. I put the phone down and Sally said, "You didn't get your way? Oh no! What are you going to do now?"

She laughed, as how many personalities does she see every day? I looked around and realized I seriously screwed up and made my bed. I was there for months. I got locked up in solitary for a day with the Bible, a piece of paper, and a pencil. I thought, *What if I stabbed myself with the pencil?* I wouldn't do it. It was only for twenty-four hours to teach me a lesson. It sucked. I can see why people would lose their mind if they were in the hole for a week!

I tried to get involved in the activities around me. One time, I broke my foot playing baseball barefoot in the field, and another time, I had to have a solid gold ring cut off my finger because I'd gained so much weight that it was cutting off my circulation. Despite everything, I kept working in the kitchen, even though the other girls would steal things from my locker while I was on shift.

I did what I could to help the new girls, trying to give back, the way Mishnaf had helped me when I first arrived. I wrote letter after letter to my family and even to my attorney, but my attorney gave up on me, hanging up the phone and leaving me to rot, even through the holidays. It was survival mode. I ate whatever I could, and I devoured book after book, losing track of how many I read.

I kept writing letters filled with remorse, hoping someone would respond. I attended self-help classes and went to art sessions to pass the time. One day, a girl came in to sing for us. I recognized her—she was clean now. I asked if she could help me get out, but she said she couldn't, as she was just a volunteer. I'd need a real rehab sponsor to make any progress.

On another day, Mishnaf and I were stuck in our room during a long lockdown for administrative reasons. She decided to lighten the mood by teaching me how to wrap a flat sheet like a Pareo, a traditional Tahitian sarong. She even tried to teach me some Tahitian dance moves. It was hilarious because I couldn't get the hang of the figure-eight motion, and without music, it was hard to find any rhythm. She started singing, but she was white, so it was a bit of a challenge to get into the whole "shake your booty, Polynesian-style" vibe. Still, we had fun, and she made me laugh—one of the few bright moments in a place that was otherwise so heavy.

I heard the guard yelling an announcement to the module. She said, "Daytop Village is here to talk to you girls. Whomever wants to attend, come to your door, and look out."

So, I asked what that was all about. Mishnaf said that it was a hard rehabilitation program that I would do well at if I was ready, but it was super hard, and that she didn't know if it was something I could handle.

She said, "If you don't make it, you return here to Rikers."

I was like, "Fuck, no!"

I heard that challenge and it piqued my curiosity, and of course, made me feel like—*Oh, someone is doubting me, huh?* I had issues with that. So, I went to the door and looked out. I was thinking—*How hard can it be?* And I figured if I didn't like it, then I'd do what

I always do. I'd figure it the fuck out. The guards let me out and I attended the presentation. I was in the front row, and I was watching this Asian guy talk. He looked awfully familiar. He kept walking back and forth and talking about how he changed his life, and then it hit me. I knew him—it was Aaron T from Vermont!

He was the drug dealer my friend and dad shipped me to to get straightened out. It was where I overdosed badly and yes, I returned to the city, but geographical changes never work for quitting dope. I was a dope magnet. No matter where I went, I could sniff it out and locate it in a heartbeat. I shouted at him from the crowd, "Hey, Aaron, how are you? Do you remember me?"

He was confused and said he didn't place me.

So, I told him, "It's me, Mariemie."

He didn't recognize me, as I had gained about fifty pounds since the last time he saw me, when I was in my teens. Of course, being in jail for a few months over the holidays and eating cup noodles at night with soda or cocoa did not help to maintain my svelte figure. Then he laughed and said, "Wow, I can't believe you are here!"

After the meeting, I was talking to him and he asked what kind of charges I had, so I told him, one Class A, one Class C, and one misdemeanor. He said that the Class A was going to interfere, as they didn't accept Class A tried felons. *The phrase that would haunt me for decades. Ugh.* So, I asked him to do what he could to help me out. I told him I didn't belong there and if he could change, so could I. He agreed and said he would be in touch.

So, this time, the jail staff changed roommates, as you are in there longer. I ended up with about three different ones after Mishnaf. I was bummed as she and I were so close. So, I met this skinny Black chick, and I came across this book that looked tattered, with a needle on it. The title was *Journey from Hell*, by Vinny

Marino. I picked it up and started reading it. I was into it, and I couldn't put it down.

She looked at me and was like, "Do you know what you're reading and who that is?"

I said I was hooked and felt like he was talking about me, that I was him. She said that if the book was doing that to me, I may be wanting to change my ways. She said it was a hard program, and knowing me, she had her doubts that I could finish it. *Here we go again, another drug addict doubting me. Don't they know that's not cool and makes me prove them wrong?* Well, then I realized this was the program Aaron T was with. *Where the fuck did that drug dealer crackhead go?*

I asked Sally if I could call Daytop Village. She said sure and started laughing at me. I asked, "Why are you laughing at me?"

She said, "I think it's funny that the worst and sassiest chick in Rikers wants to go to Daytop Village instead of taking the easy way out in jail or with a Band-Aid program for thirty days."

I said, "Those programs don't work."

"I haven't been to one, so how would I know that?"

I clarified that in Vinny's book, he explained how it didn't work, and it was a waste of time. All I knew inside was that what I was reading was the only book and solution that resonated with me, ever. I had to act on it, so I called Aaron T at the program. He said that if I wanted in, I would find a way to locate him, and I did. He and Paul, the other guy who was with him the year prior at the meeting, came to visit me each week and asked me the same questions over and over.

Are you ready? Are you done? How bad do you want this?

I was over it and kept reiterating that I was ready for a change. During this time, my sister Kate knew that I was wanting to do this, and she came to visit me. She reported back to the family but no one else came to see me, including my mom. My mom said she would go anywhere else, but not to a prison to be told to cough while squatting.

I was writing to Daytop Village and begging that they get me out of there. There were months of court proceedings, and finally, they got approval from the judge to have me on supervised release to the residential drug rehabilitation program. I was anxiously awaiting the infamous call of the inmate who is next in line to be released. A week went by, and I was still waiting. I called Daytop Village, and they finally arranged for the day I could expect them to open those doors out of hell and disgrace. That was exactly what Daytop Village wanted to see—complete desperation. I was called on that magical day and I looked around the module and said to the fellow inmates, "I'm out of here!"

I got checked out and got the funds issued to me and I said, "Let's go eat some real food before we head there." And both guys looked at each other, one being the drug dealer from upstate, and the other Todd M. They chuckled and said to me, "Any funds from you will be solely donated to the program as contribution to your treatment."

I was astounded and disappointed, and then thought, whatever, I was out of that place and on to a new beginning. Out of Rikers, with my black trash bag, no shoelaces, jeans that were too tight, and that awful Ralph Lauren sweater, weighing 152 pounds.

CHAPTER 13: DAYTOP VILLAGE, A PLACE OF CHANGE

It was a long ride through tunnels, cliffs, and then into a parking lot full of vehicles with two females sitting at what appeared to be a guard shack or stand, where residents would write in a composition book, upon verifying the spelling of your name. I waved hello to the girls there as I swung my large, hefty trash bag over my shoulder and was guided into a secret-looking hallway that led into a basement-type office. I guess I had arrived.

A man named Paul pulled out an application that was nearly ten pages long with questions only he could see. He started to ask me about topics that led me to glorify the days of being a hustler in the street, slinging dope, and manipulating others. He then had me laughing while he wrote it down on the sheets of paper, one unbelievable story after the next. It felt like it was an eternity before he called for a female named Lea. She arrived, with her long head of silver hair, and Paul asked her to take me on a tour of the female dormitory. We walked from the office below, above, and across the basketball court into the large house with the ocean view, then up the stairs.

As we went through the facility, she was introducing me to the existing residents. We got to the bathroom shower area, and I saw multiple shower heads with two stalls, and there were nearly thirty-two women at that time. I was mortified that we'd have to share showers, and she laughed and said, "No, we take turns and two go at the same time on each side." *Thank you, Jesus,* I thought! After that, she led me to a chair by a chalkboard fronting the main check-in counter where a male sat behind a small desk. He kept staring at me, and I was uncomfortable.

I had a carton of Benson & Hedges Menthol Lights that I was smoking away while I sat on the chair and watched these people who were concierges running back and forth, shouting calls to the front desk and vice versa. Meetings occurred and then the entire facility showered at the same time. They would call, "House can shower," in an extremely loud tone up and down the hallway. They didn't use intercom systems, as the residents ran the entire operation.

I saw very few staff members, and most of them were either staff trainees or were once a resident themselves. I started to feel like they forgot I was there. So, of course me and my ADHD went to the front desk without standing behind the red line to be acknowledged. I was corrected and then told I had to stand there and wait to be called upon by that man who was staring at me. I asked in the politest voice I could pull off, "May I approach the front counter, please?"

Pleased, he said, "Yes, Marie, you may."

"Have I been forgotten about?"

"I have looked at you for the past few hours, and now I realize you are there."

I chuckled and felt ridiculous, so I sat back down. I now realized that they were, for real, fucking with me. I was annoyed and it started to show. I asked for another cigarette and mentioned to the creepy guy that I had more of those and where would I be keeping them?

He said, "You don't get to keep these. You get to smoke Dorals."

I said, "I believe you are misunderstanding. I bought those in jail."

He said, "No, I am crystal clear on this. You are donating those, as well as whatever valuables you had with you, and you're not allowed to keep them while you're here."

I said, "Wait, what? Dorals? I don't understand. I don't smoke that brand of tumbleweed, and I purchased my own to bring here."

He then said, "Sorry, rules here. Tons of them. Get used to it, girl."

That was when the short Asian girl came to get me from the chair I was on for nearly three and a half hours. She led me into the house and into a room where I saw a man of color, who looked nice, along with a blonde, and the young girl asked me to sit in the chair, facing all of them. The man, H, told me to explain a bit about myself. He guided me with questions, and I crossed my legs, feeling like this was a job interview. I continued to respond and then suddenly, the little girl turned to me and started yelling at me. Then the blonde started in, and she got real down and dirty, verbally.

They were all screaming at me about what a scumbag I was and how I could be so "nonchalant" and "condescending." I was freaking out and started to cry. They liked it and continued to break me down of the guilt, sadness, and regret I had within myself. Once they saw me sobbing uncontrollably, they asked me to scream for help. *I was like, WTF?*

"To who?" I asked.

They responded by all saying, "To yourself, to the ocean, the mountains, the street, to the facility, and so everyone can hear you in this town!"

I was befuddled and asked myself—*Do you want to go back to the place you just came from? No fucking way!*

So, I started screaming from the pit of my stomach, and then what did they do? They all hugged me and said, "Welcome to the family!"

Wow. I am shocked. I am embarrassed and beside myself. I said to myself—*You fucked up hard. Boy, you are being paid back for all that shit you did on the street and to your family. You must complete this! There is no other way.*

I walked out and they helped me upstairs to the bunk beds. When you are new, you are on the top and must climb up on the edge of the metal frame. If you piss off your bunkie, you'll get looks, but one of the concepts in there is no violence allowed. So, I knew no one could act out and if they did, they'd get the chair or whatever they were doing with the guy that had his head shaved when I was on that chair during a meeting. I unpacked the only property I had to my name, which wasn't much. I asked if I could get my mom to send me clothes. They immediately said, "No, you are on your own, and you shop in the used clothes boutique that we have on the facility."

At this time, the program was being run by the original founders, who were from Little Italy. Yes, it did remind me of a "family," just like the *Sopranos* or *Goodfellas*. The clothing in the shop included T-shirts that choked your neck and were so unattractive. I was heavier, so I suppose it was best to cover up. The place was absolutely beyond clean—not one speck of dust anywhere, and the entire facility smelled like bleach and cleaners. There were people that I tried to speak with, and they were so serious and would not respond or engage with me. It was like I was invisible.

The blonde from earlier was named my older sister. She was designated as my shepherd through the fields of the confusion there. The girl with the stocking cap on her head cleaning near the front desk was carrying a bucket and I offered to hold it for her, and she looked at me and smiled and had to report herself at the front desk that she smirked at me.

I told myself this would be my home for the next three and a half years. I would see a century turn in there, with Y2K and the introduction of Microsoft loading for ten minutes when you turn on your computer. DOS was the previous system. *But I am dating myself.*

The property was an old mansion estate that was donated to the cause of the program. It had a spectacular view and a large parking lot behind the kitchen and the entryway. There was a massive restaurant-style kitchen with a spacious dining room to hold over 150 people, dry storage, walk-in fridges, freezers, professional dishwashing area, bread ovens, deep fryers—really a chef's dream. There was a fishpond with fish, turtles, and a waterfall outside. There were female, male, and staff dorms, a medical department, fitness center, pool, weight room, sauna, steam room, basketball and volleyball courts, along with hydroponic vegetable gardens.

They ran the entire operation in house with medical, accounting, HR, grants, coordinating, sales, administration, and culinary departments. They did not accept assistance from the state or federal government. They survived on grants, donations, paid rent for the wealthy residents (yes, there were famous people in there), individual residents on assistance, and then the fundraising and acquisition departments. It was a full running system that had been in business since 1971. It was completely self-sustaining and self-sufficient, and all residents were also trained to either become a staff member to give back and/or to graduate completely and be released for life on their own.

The methods were an extraction of many programs fused together to make it what it was. You had no reason to leave for anything. You were there to concentrate on yourself. It had a health element to it, and no resident was ever hungry. They fed us like kings and queens. They also issued either ten packs of chewing gum or a carton of Doral cigarettes per week, green menthol or red non-menthol. You had to stand in line and ask for it, then sign off that you were in receipt of it. You also could not hoard extra gum or cigarettes from the week prior if you were an existing resident.

The day after entry, we had to be taken to the lab so they could draw blood and test you for all communicable diseases. We had to eat outside of the dining room and on paper plates, until our results were approved. Once that clearance was issued, we were allowed to eat in the dining room on the regular dishware with the rest of the family.

There was a hot breakfast each morning that included eggs, bacon, pancakes, waffles, potatoes, and rice. The other side of the room offered a selection of dry or hot cereal, toast, yogurt, cottage cheese, and a fruit bar. I had never imagined the food was going to be of that level. I mean elevated, like we were at the Four Seasons, and they fed you two snacks in between your three large meals, which also included dessert for lunch and dinner. Plus, seconds or thirds if there was a surplus. You had all this food, and of course, it was to feed you and give you what you need, but drug addicts take it to another level when they see that buffet line—just like they did with the dope smorgasbord. You eat and eat again.

During the holidays, they had turkeys and hams on each round tablecloth-covered table of ten, along with the other nine courses for said event. We had servers who would dress up and the rest would be sitting down enjoying. I believe I only had holidays like that, as I was either kitchen or server crew. No issue there, of course. Valerie, the co-founder, taught all about Cannoli cream, Chicken Marsala, Seafood Salad. On Christmas Eve, we had Italian seafood, and on Christmas, it was meat and chicken. I learned about stuffed bread and was all too familiar with the imported food. It was ridiculous, overzealous, and so delicious. They were teaching us the family-oriented culture that had been missing in our lives while being a dope fiend. The nighttime security guards were allowed to eat special snacks, as well as ramen from the industrial-size kitchen.

There was a rigid schedule of wake-up time at 6:00 a.m. each Monday, Wednesday, and Friday as you had to go to aerobics class first, then you could eat breakfast and shower. New residents would have to participate in the day programs while the older residents went to work to run the facility in each department. We called each other our brothers and sisters. At the end of their shift, they would shower, eat dinner, and then commingle with us younger residents on the floor, as they called it.

We had meetings, rap sessions, events, and other activities that made the day go by fast. However, we were extremely tired at night and in the a.m. It was life; we were in rehab boot camp. We needed it. On Tuesdays and Thursdays, working out was optional, and then you could have breakfast in the dining room, drink coffee, and watch CNN only. We had a huge TV with a nice sound system. We knew every current event daily, but there was no local news unless there was an emergency that the founders believed we should know about. On Saturdays, we were able to get up at 8:00 a.m. and 9:00 a.m. on Sundays, only if we didn't work on the weekend in a regular job or a part-time weekend job. It was a full, real-life-in-training so that you could go from drug addict in the street with no plan or responsibility to the 9:00 to 5:00 type day. However, it was heavy therapy. It was conditioning for your brain, soul, and body to be able to survive as a sober, productive, and honest member of society. The pressure and therapy came from peers in the program. It was not quite what I had expected, but then again, I would think—*I am not in jail and no longer getting my head counted. All good. I am grateful beneath it all.*

There was a schoolroom with an older retired-looking teacher who was paid to be our homeroom and all subject teacher. It did not matter if you were eighteen, in your twenties, or even in your fifties—if you did not have your high school diploma, you had to attend the on-site school and enroll in GED classes. It was a requirement, just like how I had to obtain my driver's license. Yes, I drove illegally prior to the stint in jail. I was faced with studying for both in tandem and it was overwhelming. I hadn't been in any type of learning curriculum for over a decade, and had no desire to do it at this point in my life.

The guy of color took a liking to me and gave me an extra hard time in the rousting department. He said I needed it to be on the right path, as he could tell I was stubborn, indignant, and selfish. True, but how else was I supposed to survive on the street? He would single me out in meetings and asked me to participate in all subjects. He said he noticed I was bossy, so he made me the leader of the new resident group to draw heat to me from the fellow residents. I oversaw counting all the residents, running the meetings, and being on the creative team to organize plays that would depict a message. Then, we would act them out on stage to the rest of the family.

We had to participate in the image-breaker groups. It was described as being on stage with about forty residents staring at you, along with the staff member in charge for that day or night shift. They were typically in the morning when we were exhausted from the day prior and not in our perky moods. The audience was allowed to heckle you, and if they told you you had to act like a gorilla doing ballet with a constipation problem, then you had to do it. It was tough for some, but not me too much. I felt like a natural, and if I could make people laugh over my stupidity, why the fuck not? It was a way to goof off and not be serious for an hour, so you're damn right I was up for it. I was able to build my confidence through this activity, and I had a special Bruce Lee version of me where I would do kicks, flips, and fake karate while moving my mouth and then speaking like it is seen in the old martial arts movies. It made everyone laugh. It was so dumb, and I must have looked ridiculous. But once again, it was not lost on me that I was not scrubbing the toilets in prison. *All good.*

We had every ethnicity and demographic you could imagine—Asians, Blacks, Latinos, Italians, Greeks, Caucasians, Portuguese, celebrities, seniors, young adults, siblings, children, spouses, poor, wealthy, severe behavioral issues, and the list goes on. Everyone had a specific craft that was utilized to contribute to the need to run the facility by the resident's philosophy. The training we received was phenomenal. There were, of course, thorns in every bush, and we had folks who didn't make it—just like the girl told me in prison. I witnessed so many incidents of residents either disappearing in the middle of the night, being asked to leave or to graduate, or even put on a pause-type graduation, until they passed the tests post-graduation. It was not a cookie-cutter type of program.

We had encounter groups twice a week—some with only females and most with a mixed male and female group. The confrontations in the meetings were controlled; however, being yelled at by another drug addict was tough to digest. It was demeaning, and why not? We were all the same. At first, it was so off-putting. But at the end, I was one of the scariest people to be told off in "games," as they called it. I was grateful they chose me to join this family. It was one of the hardest times of my life. But, if you could smoke crack, shoot up heroin, or take a zillion pills and drink yourself to near death, then you could act civilized and finish the program successfully.

Accomplishments ran deep. I obtained my driver's license for the first time in 1997, *hooray*, and my GED with one of the highest scores of the group. I received two medical procedures, had two teeth pulled and others that were fixed. My mother wanted to pay to save the one tooth, and for cleanings every six months at least. I was told, “Nope, you are on your own and your mother is on a fixed income.” We ended up removing the rotten bunch that was the result of smoking too much meth and then had to wait until we moved out to be able to receive a professional cleaning, unless we saved our own money from what we earned in the program.

The first couple of years were growth. It was where I grew up as a young adult and cultivated my first set of post-drug addict friendships. During the program, I was harassed by Jesse, who would call when I was the receptionist on the main phone line. He was a former resident in the program many years past and graduated, but ended up with the wrong people who also did not make smart choices. Those were his friends, ex-residents. I would have never known this when I waited outside the homes of drug dealers, who were former residents of the program, when I was with him in years past. I found out while I was in there how the connection was.

Part of the drug raid gang also attempted to enter the program, and I begged the director and founders not to allow it—not because I didn’t want him to get help, but because I knew it was manipulation. He wanted to see with his own eyes that I made the decision to get clean. I could not be around those people, as I had truly made a significant change for the better. I was serious about my recovery. During the program, I was told from day one that I would never have contact with any of my children, and I was reminded that I gave them up and they were closed adoptions with rescission, or right thereof. This was a challenge for me as I had to watch others be able to visit with their kids, and it was a constant reminder of how fucked I was to choose dope over my little humans that I gave birth to. No matter what and how much I changed, I could cry at the drop of a dime if anyone brought them up or if I had deeper thoughts of them. H noticed this depressed me and interfered with my direction and goals. So, he clipped the convos and made it a hard rule, no one was to bring up my children, in any rap sessions, group settings like games, in casual conversation, or likewise. It was like they never existed.

In 1999, my whole world changed. The founder of the program became sick with an illness that he fought like a champion for years until it took him out. The facility and co-founder, his wife, was devastated. The vibration of the facility was sensitive, and the mood was dark. During this time, my mom would not have much to say about my brother Brad when she called. I would ask, and she would not be able to say anything negative, as that was against the program policies. Hard rules that could cost me connection with my family or banned visits. I was not willing to take that chance, so I did not press the issue. All positivity to each resident on every visit and phone call.

It would interfere with the resident's program if we allowed negative family matters, and so whomever covered my call was not allowed to discuss this business about Brad. I had bad vibes, like visions that were unexplainable. Hurt, remorse, and sadness came over me one day. I pulled Eden aside and told her that I had a bad feeling my brother was going to die. She asked why I thought that, and I said I didn't know. On July 13, 1999, I was pulled into the back office I was interviewed in. I was told by H and two other girls to sit down.

I asked, "What is going on?"

H said, "Marie, your brother committed suicide."

I took my glasses off and tears shot out of my eyes. The room went black. My soul left my body, and I just lost my shit all over the place. I begged H to tell me that he was still alive, but possibly in the hospital, and H said, "I am sorry, Marie. He's gone."

I ran out to the area where we would meditate and cried so hard over and over. I rocked back and forth uncontrollably. I was in shock. *Why could I not save him? Why did he not say goodbye?* My friend found me on the bench, but I could not stop crying. My friends/sisters in there held me for hours. I don't think I ever cried that much in my entire life. I woke up and thought it was a nightmare repeatedly. I just felt so fucking sick inside. *I can honestly say it was the worst death I had ever had to deal with to date. The saddest and most pitiful goodbye.*

Three months later, my Russian dad, Billy, passed away from a long battle with congestive heart failure. That year was horrifying. I thought I would never be the same again and I wasn't. We lost the founder and then I lost the only two men who loved me to death in my life. My mother was so grief stricken. I could not leave the program as I had committed to being a staff trainee and to extend my program to get additional training under my belt. I wanted to be all the more confident and leave the program with a larger amount of funds. Prior to this, while I was hearing of my dad's illness, I was able to see him one last time prior to him passing. He witnessed me sober and was so proud. I am beyond grateful for that! It was a struggle for the better part of my life. Remember, I smoked crack at thirteen years young. This, I believe, was a massive turning point. The next year would be my last in this program. I was ready to hit the pavement and see if I could, in fact, make it without being in a supervised situation. The events in our life shape who we become.

In 2000, I was entrusted to leave the facility and started to visit my family often. My mom was depressed and sad every time I spoke with her, as Bruce was her favorite, aside from me. I had to get out there and spend time before she was gone. So, I expressed my desire to live off the facility and at a nearby sibling's house. I had to catch the city bus back and forth to the program, but I resided at my sister's, where she only lived Monday through Friday of each week.

She stayed at her boyfriend's house with her son all weekend. I had the house to myself from Friday to Sunday night, sometimes Monday. Jennifer would take me with her when I first moved in, and I would go begrudgingly. I really wanted to just lay down at the beach, or in the yard, and meditate to find my soul again. I lost my brother to dope and suicide. An epic fail again on my part, not to be there to help him escape his demons. His favorite song was "Free Bird" by Lynyrd Skynyrd, and I had the chorus carved on his urn. I loved him so much.

I graduated in October of 2000, officially. It was an accomplishment. I left with nearly $3,500—enough for a rent deposit, utilities, food, and transportation, until I had cash flow from a 9:00 to 5:00 job. While I was living at my sister's, I had to witness something so painful happen at least once a week. I gave up my three children (heartbreaking to this day), with the last one at that time being in 1993, when I had to leave my third baby in the hospital. I had been told that if I tried to remove him from there or if I didn't leave him alone from the hospital, I would have been arrested. So, this child we speak of was then around the age of seven. He was adopted by the famous athlete through Jennifer, my sister, who I no longer speak with.

I was staying with her, her friend, and her husband, who adopted my baby son. The couple could not have a baby. They found out I had a handsome boy that was of Italian descent, and one day I picked up the phone and said, "Hello?"

A boy with a raspy voice like mine came on the line and said, "Can I speak with Aunty Jennifer?"

I said that she wasn't home. I had chills running down my spine as I knew it was my child talking to me, and I was forewarned in rehab that I was to never contact nor attempt to contact as they were all closed adoptions. To everyone else, I was no longer their mother. I relinquished all rights as a parent.

He asked who I was, and I had to tell him I was an Aunty too. He didn't think anything of it, but I hung up and sobbed. I could not even acknowledge, say hello, or engage in a conversation with my own child. I had to take the message and then convey to the cold sister who basically made that agreement, knowing I'd never be a part of his life. Each week I lived there, I saw this kid more and more. He would get out of the truck with his dad and walk to his mom's office that was in the back of this house that I was residing in. I could not deal with it anymore. I had to move away to my own place, so I started looking for roommates.

Can you imagine seeing your child, who you gave up, with no rights to touch him or say hello? But I was allowed to peek out the window and look. They said that was okay. *Get the fuck out of here!*

CHAPTER 14: THE PI, SUMMA CUM LAUDE, AND REAL ESTATE

I moved into a condo with H, the director of the rehab program I was in. I went from the country into downtown Manhattan and was living in the Chinatown district, of all places, in a high rise with security. There were drug deals, prostitutes, and peopled getting merced right downstairs. I was, however, five minutes from where I worked for the private investigator firm—one of the largest in the state. I also enrolled in full-time business college with my own funds and lending. I had no vehicle, just the city bus, and worked daily while I attended full-time night school. I stayed out of trouble and was in bed each night by 11:30 p.m. and then up again at 6:00 a.m. and off to work and school five days and nights a week. I had homework at night and on the weekend, mid-terms, and finals each semester. It was during this time that I met my then boyfriend, who would become my husband. He was also a resident in the same program. He had had an addiction with heroin.

I was on the bus one day when I saw an old friend. He took my number and said he was going to give it to Max, another graduate I was friends with. I connected with Max, and he suggested we hook up since it was healthy to hang out together as alumni. I tried to set him up with a friend from the program, but he did not want to be around her. He had fun with me. But he was nearly eight years younger than me. We started hanging out as friends and then soon dated on a regular basis, but mostly kept it a secret. My mom knew and she loved him and said, “He’s going to be the best you’ll ever find.”

We moved in together after both of us didn't quite like who we were living with. My roommate undressed wherever he felt like it, and he brought home a different girl each night. *How did I know this?* They all had different size feet, and I would see their shoes on the way out of the house in the morning. (I had a no shoe rule in the house.) And his roommate gave me the creeps. I caught him nodding out when I went to use the bathroom in the middle of the night. He was burning holes in the sofa. *Hmm.* I told Max. Then we saw a small cap of a bottle upside down filled with water, cotton, a needle, and a lighter. That was all we needed to convince us that it was time we went out on our own as a couple. We didn't want to be part of the riff raff, so we moved into the only place we could afford, the ghetto.

It was not long after September 11, 2001, and we were changing direction as my hospitality career tanked once the hotels shut down from the tragedy. It was no big deal for me to reside in low-income areas as I used to do it all the time, but Max was from a nice upper middle class, Southern Baptist, Republican family (yes, they do drugs too). So, it was interesting times ahead. We had one vehicle, which he drove most of the time, and I was, of course, riding the city bus. I continued to go to school and work full-time and he enrolled in the same school to study and be near me after he was at work. We rode home together at the end of the night and discussed school things. He worked and traveled, and I stayed at home most times and went to the beach. At the time, my mom started to kick up her traveling around the world, as my stepdad had early onset dementia, so her days of freedom were numbered. This went on for a couple years at this apartment where we were near the TB clinic, and there was a lot of violence outside our door.

Cars would get in accidents and crash into our guardrail outside our bedroom window. The hood was filled with unsavory people, minus the gay couple downstairs. We were so sick of finding the washers and dryers always broken, so I had to schlep the laundry to the laundromat in a truck and all my shit would get wet on the way home as it would rain. I was volunteering at the rehab and then we had a nice sober life of basics—going to the movies, cooking, and eating out when we could afford it. His parents were wealthy, but we wanted to be on our own and not have to answer to anyone. We were proving we could do it on our own and while we were sober. I came home one day and asked if we could buy a condo. He didn't believe it was realistic and shook his head. But he quickly changed his mind after a teenager put his entire arm through a glass window downstairs—a known drug dealer's house. We were looking at townhouses the following weekend.

In 2003, I graduated from business college with a 4.0 GPA, 100% attendance for three years, no tardies, and awards for best professional image. *Gee, not bad for a high school dropout, derelict, felon, on probation.* I had been released early from probation after my attorney and I requested it in court. It was granted, and the judge said sternly, "Marie, do not backslide. You're released."

My attorney told me outside of the courtroom that if I saw anyone from my past, I needed to turn in the opposite direction and never look back. I took her advice, as I did see people and most didn't recognize me as this square. They were probably still too high anyway. One guy saw me once at a movie theater and came after me to say hello. I let the doors close and looked down and acted like he didn't exist. It was what I had to do no matter what. I was no longer that Marie. I was a new, much healthier version of myself—someone I was actually starting to like.

The PI firm was a very cool job. I entered as a lower-tiered employee and left in 2005 after working my way up to the Pre-Employment and Tenant Screening Manager. I saw so many cases that involved infidelity, murder, abuse, corrupt politicians, asbestos and lead insurance claims, location cases, and so much more. I truly learned everything there was to know about a small business. It was there that I developed my baseline in accounting, human resources, marketing, management, research, and understanding that I had to trade so much of my time for money. It wasn't clear at that time. I felt accomplished and worked my tail off from start to finish. I remained in touch with the owners, and they were very grateful to gain me as an employee and vice versa.

In 2002, we found a townhouse that was two stories and included two parking stalls—a miracle in the city! The sellers were asking $282,000. We were appalled and could not wrap our head around how we would be able to qualify and sustain the mortgage. Interest rates were 5.75% for a single-family home at the time. Max and I pulled all our resources together, as we were also engaged at that time and saving for the wedding and our future. We managed to use our savings, along with his inheritance from his grandma, and put a 20% down payment. We were grateful to receive a gift from his parents. It was our first place! *So exciting!*

The monthly mortgage payment was lower than if we were paying rent for the same place as tenants. The HOA fees did add to it, and we realized that we would be paying more if we stayed there versus a new single-family home without HOA fees. This was the start of our real estate investing and my career as an independent investor. At that time, it was a big deal for us. We soon found ourselves purchasing a single-family home that was $458,000, which I found online myself. It was not without its issues. We closed in 2004. In 2006, we had our first and only baby together. We were a family of three with two cats, and enjoyed our time at this house. It was our home for ten years, and I trained myself on construction and real estate from practical application and by asking tons of questions to experts in the field. The renovations became my new hobby and passion.

In 2013, we purchased our second home and first investment property in another county. During this time, we renovated our primary residence like we were going to live there forever. We told our parents we'd never move out of that house. In this residence, we overengineered and upgraded the entire property—everything from landscaping to plumbing to bathrooms and painting to Italian porcelain, granite, natural stone, gutters, pest control, photovoltaic, and a fucking kitchen for $98,000. We added a water feature like they have in the hotels with lights that required gloves to change out the bulbs. Our home was in the Parade of Homes in 2013, and even the original owners paid to come in and see it. They said it was unrecognizable!

I am not boasting and being conceited. This was a massive undertaking, and I loved every single second of it. I mean, it was my passion. I felt like I was Marie the builder in some other life. I found that it was truly an activity I thoroughly enjoyed. Now, don't get me wrong—drywall dust and the shitty part of construction and being exposed to it all while living in the same house sucks. But it still wasn't bad for two ex-dopeheads that were near death before. God wanted us around, and I believe it was to spread the word and help others. I realized during this time of healing that no one had a gun to my head to be a drug addict. We hold the cards, and we are in the driver's seat, always, even if it doesn't feel that way at times. It's a choice, and once I was taught to flip the switch and do good with the motivation I had as I did on the street, I was on that train, and I never stopped. I may get knocked off course, and I get right back on and go full speed ahead.

While the real estate was happening, our careers had catapulted into the next level. Max went from being a GM at a construction company to a software engineer earning double what he was at the former company. I was promoted to General Manager of an environmental hazardous waste company, multiplying the millions for the boss I had then. After nearly ten years at the company, I was beyond miserable, exhausted, and not being paid as much as I had been in years prior. Completely mistreated and undervalued, I began to experience depression, and before going into my house, I'd cry in my driveway for 15-20 minutes until I was able to not tear up when I saw my youngest son, Garrett.

I was in a job where I had worked so hard to become the highest level of management, and was sad at the same time. Max said that they had opportunities in his industry in other states, and maybe it was time to explore. I was not in agreement with this at first. However, after looking at the homes and elevated lifestyle versus where we were, I realized the hamster wheel was in full effect, and it was dang expensive for so little in return. Max believed it'd be easy for me to locate work with my experience, and he'd be making enough money, so I could work part-time, take care of our son and my family, and focus on building my small business.

So, I joined a multi-level marketing nutrition company that was helping people get healthy and lose weight. I studied to be a health coach and took the necessary courses and received Certificates of Completion online. I had an eating disorder my whole life. I was body conscious since I was a teenager, as my mom obsessed with her weight and figure, which became an issue if I did not apply discipline. Remember, Japanese Warrior shit. Imagine the butler on *Mr. Deeds,* and then a small ninja warrior with white hair and nice skin. That's her. My contractors who performed work at our residence were afraid of her. She's ninety-two and looks like a seventy-five-year-old. She still cooks, cleans, does laundry, gardens, and takes care of five animals.

Back to my career, or lack thereof. It was a time of feeling saturated. I was longing for something else. I discussed my feelings with Max, and he encouraged me, as he always does, to not be afraid and take chances. We started to explore properties all over. We were pondering life away from our home. We shared our thoughts with my daughter, who was now back in my life, and she expressed that she was unhappy in her relationship with her boyfriend from fucking hell. He was like the Devil Incarnate's cousin—one of the worst people I've ever known in my life (and that is saying a lot). He was the definition of a scumbag. Imagine a Ninja Turtle, but an ugly one, with shark eyes and huge feet that stomped like fee, fi, fo, fum, a slob when he eats, and a pervert who snorts coke.

I was still working at the hazmat company, and that boss, while he gave me so much in monetary value, didn't appreciate me as a human being. He felt like I owed him. In the back of my mind, I continued to ponder moving from the state to start a new life with endless opportunities. We started our search and decided on a trip to a state east of the Rockies. We planned a trip with my daughter, Garrett, and Max to California Disneyland as a reward vacation after we shopped for homes. We looked at fifty properties in five days and decided on the fiftieth one. We put the earnest deposit of $10,000 down and signed documents to buy the home. Then we headed to Disneyland, and it was there, at the tail end of the trip, that I started to see another side of my daughter.

CHAPTER 15: THE RESIGNATION TO THE 2ND DEVIL INCARNATE

We returned from the house hunting and Disneyland trip, perplexed with too much to deal with due to the impending move. Max got an offer to keep his job at the firm and they offered to pay for our move in full, including our car and all our belongings. We were so stoked, but I had anxiety about putting in my notice at my job. The Devil was going to make my last few months there miserable, as he was all about the head games. I was scared as I had built wealth and cultivated relationships in an industry and community for decades. And for the ten years prior, I was a successful GM that made multi-millions for the two companies the Devil owned. It was time for a new chapter, as I was beyond burnt out. I felt like my soul was torn out of my chest.

I took my boss out to lunch at his favorite place where they have good seafood. We sat down and I looked out at the water. Then, I told him my news. "I am moving to another state."

He looked up at me and laughed. "Are you joking?"

"No. This is for real and it's happening in less than two months. I am giving you nearly eight weeks advance notice to resign."

He excused himself from the table—apparently, to go vomit. *Wow, I had that much of an effect on him.* But I was starting to feel that I was meant for much more than this and to build my own dream, not his. I just didn't know it yet for sure. He was about to lose his most prized employee. I did everything for that guy. I was his EA, PA, GM—all the fucking acronyms. He paid me well and helped me with my real estate career. He also took much of it back toward the end and I was treated like all the other people he didn't like.

But it is always best to find the silver lining in every situation. And it's always there, if you look. We moved in 2014 and have been where I am now ever since. I am happy and grateful; I made the leap. I gained confidence from a therapist who said, "Try it and if it doesn't work out, you can always return home." In ten years, I saw more growth than in my whole life before. I truly understand where wisdom comes from. I learned so much about business from this guy, and while I was unhappy at times, I returned the favor many years later when his son passed away from a drug overdose. I was there for him and his family like always, and I know he'll never forget that. I also ran his company for pennies on the dollar and once again, made him a fuck ton of money in a very short amount of time with less expenses. That's a win. Anything is possible (*AIP).

We arrived at our new home in 2014, and we were wiped out. The snow and weather in New York are much different than dry, colorful Colorado. There is hardly any humidity in high elevation, which means no bugs. There is the best snow to ride on, a higher-level education, abundance, better medical care, and more house for your money. At the time we moved, there were thousands of people fleeing California or the West Coast and moving to Colorado. It was one of the first states to legalize marijuana. The influx of new residents into the state caused property values to rise and taxes to follow. We were just testing the waters at this point in the world of real estate. Honestly, it was truly a culture shock, and I mean no disrespect to anyone who is a local or moved here many moons ago. The demographic is extreme in the different counties, neighborhoods, and income levels. The education system is excellent, and tough if you have a child who was not learning at that level, even at the same grade. The Colorado Rockies are magnificent and majestic. A terrific place for a brand-new start and opportunities. We were so excited. We are still amped, jazzed, and tickled pink.

I had been trading my time for money, which is what most people in the world do at a J.O.B., building someone else's dream. It's voluntary, and no one has us chained to the desk or has a gun to our heads—that was the old Marie!

In 2014, I had been sober since 1996. We drank occasionally—six years post-graduation from rehab. My husband had his software engineer position with a stable income. Most importantly, he enjoyed what he did. I, on the other hand, felt stuck and lost. I moved away from a place where I grew up with family, friends, and an entire life with so many memories. It was home. At that time, feeling comfortable and retiring were the objectives we were striving for, as that's what our elders have programmed us to do. That was the American Dream. I get it; however, I couldn't keep still. To me, it sounded awful to retire and flail through life. My husband still wanted it, and I had no problem with it as long as I could be the one making moves. I had spent decades unlearning what had been taught and what had sunk into my subconscious. *If you don't understand that, you must Google the Bob Proctor stick person, and a YouTube video on it will come up. Watch it, understand it, and watch it again until you do. It's very simple, yet complex. If it weren't for it, they would not have come from the formless substance. (Look that up as well.)*

I arrived in Colorado, still connected to the W2 J.O.B. It was to be a remote position, and I had the company VOIP system phone hooked up, so it rang in my office at home. The entire setup worked, and while this was going on, I decided to build out the unfinished basement. I vetted, hired, contracted, and managed all the contractors and vendors that serviced any of our properties. That fell voluntarily in my wheelhouse. My husband hated that realm, and I loved it, so it was a win-win.

I embarked on expanding my network marketing business while I worked for the boss virtually. I met tons of people through these activities all over the state. I learned to drive on the I25, I225, I70W and I70E, 470 East and West, Hwy 36, Hwy 285, Hwy 24, and more. This was a miracle, as I was not ambitious to drive on the freeways with the needling of the Cali drivers that moved here. Throw snow and ice in the mix with heavy winds and hail, and you have catastrophe if you're in the wrong place at the wrong time. This was real weather, and now I know why all those travelers in the wagons died many years ago when crossing the Rockies and going West. Good Lord, it is tricky here with the tripolar weather.

We were settling in, and the tension was growing from the Boss Devil Wears Prada, but I ignored it as it was nearing the holidays. We love Thanksgiving. Why do we celebrate it over and over? We are thankful we are not poking the fun house mirror, peeing in a toilet with no seat, getting mobbed by inmates, or in rehab doing the constipated gorilla, even though we are thankful for that opportunity. We celebrate our new lives in our lovely dining room, with the niceties that we can afford and a badass brined four-day organic turkey with all the fixings and sides you can imagine. At that time, we drank, so it was all the finest wine, vodka, and beer one would want. We loved having people over, and our neighbors are the bomb dot com. Christmas is my husband's favorite, and he is a close second to Clark Griswold. All the normal things sober people do. We loved it. It was awesome. And block parties for New Year's to ring in the…

On January 15, 2015, Mr. Devil Wears Prada called me to say, "It's not really working out, is it?"

I said, "In what way?"

After that, it was like the voices in the Charlie Brown movies, and all I could hear was blah, blah, fucking blah. He tried to offer a $10,000.00 severance, no ten-year watch like he promised (I don't wear watches too much, anyhow) and no unemployment or benefits. He said that I had $3,000.00 in my 401k. *What?* I joined his company in 2005, and by 2011, we were at nearly ten million annually. He and his partner split with the worst divorce I've ever witnessed, and I was dragged through that, assisting with the closure and reopening of company two. I babysat his son, ordered and coordinated catering for two funerals, convinced his ex-wife to sign his prenuptial, cleaned his house, hired his staff, sold his cars and personal effects, golfed with Asian guys that were boring, and became the face of that hazmat company. And he pays me that as a fuck you? *Oh, hell no.*

So, I filed for unemployment, and I got it for six months. I took the $10,000.00 and transferred my $3,000.00 401k and said, "Good luck in your endeavors, motherfucker."

And, to my satisfaction (I know it's not nice), but he's never been able to make what he made when I left, which was six million per year. He turned a profit when I was there. He made, at best, $1.9 million consecutively post-Marie departure, and profit was done each year with expenses through the roof and his life out of control. Accounting reports don't lie, and I can say with conviction, I was a badass motherfucker. There is no bitterness.

CHAPTER 16: COOK STREET AND A WEEKEND WITH BOB PROCTOR

I was pondering life and, of course, deciding on a career path, while I continued to build my small business. We had one rental in Jersey with an ex-Vet staying there. We didn't make money, but it paid the mortgage, and the house was appreciating each year. I signed up for culinary classes and was having fun, pairing wine with food, cooking on an elevated level, and meeting new people every day. It was stimulating, but the money and success weren't there.

I felt like I was forever climbing up a hill and then falling back down. I worked at my friend's bar and restaurant with a loud nightclub and soon found that it's not as much fun being on the service side of the crowd. I hated it and it was tough work. I started to look at my administration side and believed it was time to open up a limited liability company and do my best to offer concierge and assisting services. I registered the business, opened bank accounts, and marketed my services. I was getting some business, just not enough, and was becoming exhausted with all these networking groups. I felt like I was wasting my time and losing money. I felt stuck once again, and this time, I couldn't blame anyone but myself. It's really always yourself!

I was on social media one day and I saw a clip of the leader of our team with the legendary Bob Proctor. I was not familiar with him. She was so excited and on fire, and he's in the background smiling, and she has just paid him nearly $50,000.00 to train directly with him. I was blown away and didn't understand the concept. I didn't get it at all. She announced there would be this huge event, called "The ABCs of Success." It was a weekend in Los Angeles with this man and his team at a live event. She paid for two tables of ten and wanted her teammates to buy them and come to the event. It included one meal per day in the hotel in the nice dining room, refreshments, water, tea and coffee, plus a bag of his favorite books. I asked around in Colorado about this man, and an older woman from a networking group said, "That's the guy that is in *The Secret*."

The Secret? What's this fucking secret?

"It's a movie," she told me.

Oh, okay. So, in my mind, I was hearing, *you must go*, and on the other hand, I felt like I was going to spend the weekend with this hokey man and this Secret. I was thinking negatively, apprehensive, and yet I went.

I arrived at the hotel, checked in, and was about to take my bag to the room when I heard a noise, and everyone was lining up like the Stones were at the hotel. I looked over and saw familiar faces. It was the networking girls, so I hooked up with them and they told me that we needed to get to the dining room where Bob was.

"That older man from *The Secret* is awake right now and starting the seminar? Get the fuck outta here?!"

Some of us who arrived later still had our luggage, and we just wheeled it into the dining room with us. I looked around. The ballroom had a huge sound system, the tables were full of people, the hotel staff were running around, and everyone was dressed up. I was glad I wore my nice cocktail dress, because I thought I would go to have wine at the bar, eat a late snack, go to bed, and be at the seminar at 9:00 a.m. That was not the case. The start of "The ABCs of Success" was on Friday night, when we literally just arrived. I was tripping. I took a seat and then the video rolled out, and eventually, *The Secret* man, Bob, walked out.

He was older but dressed to the nines! He was confident, seemed nice, and he had a glow around him that I can't even explain. He was THE (I know, the potty mouth) motherfucking man! He had to have this Secret. He totally looked the part. He began to speak, and I was immediately captivated beyond measure. He proceeded to tell all in the room something to the effect of, "I bet all of you thought the seminar started tomorrow."

He asked for a raise of hands, and I put my hand up. He further stated that they, at the Proctor Gallagher Institute, do not start the next day. "The time is now."

I was enthralled, and my eyes never moved off him. I watched it all and listened to every word he said. I was on *fiyah* (fire) for the first time in a long time. In fact, this was different. This ignited the pilot light that had been blown out for all these years. I wrote in the notebook they gave us, and I still have it to this day. I write in it when I study Bob. The book has memories that it works and the vibration that makes me feel complete. I leave and I am shaken. This old man has me more turned on than Bon Jovi! *What the fuck is going on here?* I go up to my room and I can't sleep. I want to go jog around the block and yell that I am happy again! *What is this Secret? I want some!*

I took a selfie that night on my hotel bed and I have it still. You can see a golden rose glow on my face. I was thrilled to see him for the next two days. The weekend was nothing short of perfect. He dazzled all of us. On the last day, Sunday, I got to the room early. They were not ready to start, and I heard sound checks and there was some issue. I peeked my head in the large doors and there he was on stage in a beige suit that fit him well. He was talking to the guy across the room and testing 1, 2, 3. He looked at me as I was walking toward him. He said, "Hello, how are you?"

I was dying inside like it was Mick Jagger, but better. I jumped on stage, and I said, "Thank you for clearing the clouds. I am so happy I came, and I apologize if I doubted anything."

He chuckled, and I said, "I feel stuck, and I need to hear something today that'll turn that light on."

He said, "As a matter of fact, I am going to talk about feeling stuck today. You will love it!"

He then asked what I did and what brought me there.

"Network marketing."

He asked, "Do you like network marketing?"

I replied, "I don't know if I do."

He said, "Listen today, and I am sure you will hear what you need to."

Sandy Gallagher, his partner, came up to the stage and signaled it was time to begin. He asked her to hold on while he gave me his wife's cell phone number. He wanted me to call her about network marketing. During that day, he did cover being stuck and he asked the magic question: "What is it that you really want?"

Such a simple question, yet thought-provoking. I was perplexed. A girl across the table who was a member of our team said to me that maybe diving into real estate investing would be smart, as I seemed to be good at it. She wasn't wrong. Another subject he covered was writing books. He had bestselling author, Peggy McColl, a Stevie Nicks of the same world, in Bob's inner circle. She was at the next table with a pilot who wrote a book, and was close to being offered a contract from Warner Bros. I had always thought about writing a book, but I never knew where to begin.

I asked Peggy at the next table, "I'd like to do this. Do you write the book if we tell you a story?"

She said, "You have to write the book."

I giggled and realized that was a dumb question. I didn't get it then. I was forty-five at that time. Remember, I grew up late, so my maturity levels were beyond the normal curve. What do they say at the pediatrician's office? All children develop at their own pace and milestones. I left the seminar with a vibration I had never felt in my life until then. I was so happy and grateful I met that man and all the people in that realm that weekend. It was life-changing and moved me spiritually. My hair is still standing up on my arms. What a blast!

I returned home with the compounding momentum of Bob's frequency. I was confident and said to my husband, "Max, I want a house in the mountains."

He said, "Okay, how do we get it if you don't have a regular job?"

"I don't know, but we will own this house."

He believed me and thought it was a dream that might happen in a few years. But on December 5, 2015, we became the proud owners of a house in the mountains that was nearly 3,000 square feet, with multiple floors, and on land with natural alkaline water from the aquifers beneath us. We still own it to this day, and it is absolutely, positively magnificent! We are now owners of three properties. Hard work, effort, and pulling from the formless substance is where it is at. How did we get it? We found the way, as it was a burning desire. I imagined it. We drove through the mountains. I looked online all day and night for weeks. I made deals with the realtor and sellers, and our offer was accepted above another that was in escrow. Everyone in the transaction was happy. That was five months after "The ABCs of Success" and meeting Phil Goldfine, Mick Peterson, and Peggy McColl, plus many others. It was, by far, my numero uno life saver. Thank you, Bob, Spirit, and the Universe, for making it come together. I pat myself on the back for never giving up and believing in myself. For getting outside my comfort zone and diving into the Secret. Not the movie, but the sauce of the teachings.

Not only did I meet those people, but I had the courage to reach out to my third son. The one who was left at the hospital. Yes, him. I found him on Facebook, and I ripped the Band-Aid off and told myself that he could tell me to fuck off or maybe say hi. *Just do it.* I opened up the messenger, and shaking, I messaged my son, who never met me since he was two years old, never saw me peeking at him through the window at Jennifer's house, and never saw me in passing, although we lived in the same town for most of his life until we moved in 2014.

I typed, "Do you know who this is?"

He replied, "My mommy."

I almost fell back on my chair. I teared up and couldn't believe he had accepted me and called me his mommy, after all those years, the hospital incident, the years I didn't get clean, and the list goes on. He continued to communicate and sent me pictures of the professional sport he has done since he was a child. He is athletic, handsome, and has a smile that lights up the room. We stay in contact, and life is going well and only improves. My heart is warm, and my life is peaceful. I have arrived at this next level that I manifested. Thank you, Lord, the Universe, and my teachers. Without you, I would not be here today to remind all that anything is possible (AIP).

Wise
Marie
by Natasha Brune
VOLUME 1

EXCERPTS FROM VOLUME II

2018: Marie walks in the room of the NICU and sees her grandson, whose skin has turned a pale gray, with about twenty nurses, doctors, and emergency personnel all around him. They push them out of the way and focus on him. The little guy is nearly nine months old, and the oxygen mask fits snugly over his little face. He looks so tired. He's awake, but seems to be half asleep. He is limp and lifeless, yet you can see he is trying to fight.

The doctor turns to Marie and asks how long this should go on for. "When are we going to realize it is a circle?"

"Is he in pain?" she asks, tears running down her face.

"The worst kind. He is on morphine."

Marie calls, but no one answers. She is panicking. She's in town for a business trip and made time to visit—or say goodbye, it seems. Marie is sick inside and feels there is a reason she is there. Thirty minutes go by, and a young lady runs in to the lifeless baby. She cries and begs God not to take him away. A long night is ahead…

2019: A high-speed chase is happening on the Garden State Parkway in New Jersey. The cops are chasing a Mini Cooper with a young man inside. He's driving 100+ miles per hour. The police can't catch him. He pulls over, ditches the car, and runs through an affluent neighborhood until he is caught and captured, then taken to the Behavioral Hotel for 30 days. It is here we learn about the pink meth, the Balinese Mafia, shells as large as your hand, and how the food is perfect on the dark side of Islands in Bali.

2021: It is the heart of the Covid-19 pandemic. The food was prepared and left in the oven or fridge. There was much encouragement to eat these dinners. Unexplainable illnesses and not being able to walk, similar to the Osage tribe and the effects of laced culinary treats. The plans are in place to take over the compound, dispose of the waste, and inherit the estate. The drug use is intense. Lies and deceit are everywhere. Marie has found that she is back with the squalid, only this time, she didn't backslide; it's a conspiracy from the Man and Child #1 of the Korn. He has returned with a vengeance and a partner in crime. The apple does not fall far from the tree…

A NOTE FROM THE AUTHOR

I have had thoughts of writing this story for years now, only to dismiss it, as it seemed ridiculous. *Who would want to hear my tale?* Well, the moment came to me in a world crisis with the Coronavirus pandemic. It was May of 2020, and my family was in the Midwest and had been inside since March 14. That difficult time proved to be a learning opportunity for me. It allowed me to reflect that not only did I want to get this story out, but I needed it for my own well-being—for my very soul. I knew that even if one other person could identify with something in this book that would be helpful for them to use in their life, that would be the ultimate Karma.

This book is meant to provide some visualization with the surroundings, historical events, and path that was taken to move forward and leave behind the shattered pieces. It could have easily gone the other way, and I am happy to have written this, as it has proven to be a healthy piece of therapy for me.

If you or a loved one are in an abusive relationship, I know how I felt and I can only say, we're like a brother and sister from another mother or father, in that we share a common denominator—experiencing some form of abuse. Get a person to talk to. Read, write, and further your career. Create self-worth and an unstoppable image. You can do it!

Female or male humans who have been abused mentally, emotionally, or physically, or who have witnessed another person being tormented, have Post-Traumatic Stress Disorder (PTSD) that no one outside this world would understand. Watching someone kill another person or a soldier fighting for his life is PTSD, right? That's what Dr. Buzz said. Yes. However, just imagine a girl who has long, beautiful hair, and has to watch as someone takes a knife and slices off a few inches and throws it across the room. Will she ever get her hair back? Yes. Can it be fixed or grow back? Sure. How about her heart that was ripped in half? Nope. That is the part of the PTSD puzzle that connects us all. There may be various levels of PTSD, but it's the same. Post-traumatic stress disorder. It's real, people, and it sucks.

So, read the book, digest the information, and know that we do this together, one step at a time. We must break the cycle of abuse and lay our own walkway through life to the light at the end of the tunnel. There is a light. I promise. It seems so far away and it's not easy, but it's close enough. If we choose, we will win. The finish line is right there. And then we can do so much more. For example, my goal was to one day start a nonprofit organization to help other abused people learn how to remove themselves from the relationship or situation and start a brand-new, rewarding life. Fast forward to the next volume, and I will say this has already happened. There goes that formless substance again.

There are a ton of self-help books out there. I have a few that stand out in my library. You must use what works for your position and time in life—what resonates and is in harmony with YOU. At the time I was in that dark space or spaces, I didn't read a thing. My mind and emotions were full of despair and turmoil. So, maybe a friend will read this and pass it on or give you some ideas based on highlights. However it moves through the channel, I'll be satisfied. Maybe a screenplay, movie, or Netflix documentary—#manifestit.

As you get further along in the improvement phase of your life, you will want to work on larger goals. In 2015, I attended a Bob Proctor seminar over the course of a few days in Los Angeles. A friend convinced me it would be a life-changing experience and healthy to incorporate into my sales position at the time. I thought it was going to be hokey, but the first night after I went to my hotel room, I was in amazement. I dropped on my bed and was in awe. I could not believe that a man in his seventies could move me equal to or more than my rock stars that I love to see perform at a good concert. This was different. This hit a nail on the head like never before. It struck chords within me that I never knew I had. A frequency or power to beyond. What I learned in that one weekend changed my life forever and helped me get "unstuck." I bought another house a few months later and I didn't even have a consistent income. It still befuddles me how I just stepped out of my comfort zone and took those chances. Amen. It works. Anything is possible (AIP).

So, if Mary Morrissey, Bob Proctor, or another figure motivates you, then yes, I would highly suggest following that person and/or the lessons they've left behind. You are who you hang around with. If you surround yourself with those that will go nowhere, nor have the desire, then guess where you're going? Yes, you guessed it, the same place. Stagnant is a great word to describe the situation in a pool of the squalid—like the water that doesn't flow and that mosquitos breed in—you will swim in that forever. A hamster on a wheel, indefinitely. Looking at the same day over and over, like in *Groundhog Day*. Remember that movie with Bill Murray? My ADHD couldn't stand it. Do you know why? Because I like to move forward and not in a circle. I get dizzy like that. I don't like rollercoasters, even though the world is full of them, on and off the track.

It's entirely up to you. I went from being as poor and pathetic as can be, abused, on drugs, homeless, in prison, then in a residential drug rehabilitation facility, to owning businesses that brought in multiple streams of income, and the nonprofit that was my goal during the lockdown. I turned the force within me to move in the positive direction. In any situation you experience in life, always remember the good or what positive bit of knowledge you walked away with. This helps ease the pain and allows you to feel less bitter and to move on in your life to experience all four quarters, like in a football game. You saw that I did this throughout the book in various chapters, even when it was dark. I know that I can either hang onto the soul-ripping drama, or I can put it in my toolbox of experience, and it will add to my IQ and shape more of me.

Stand up and say, "I got this, bitch! I am who I am today from all of it. I have applied all the energy that I used to put into being negative in years past and turned it into a firework that exploded into another realm." I have my days of depression, sadness, and mental challenges, but that's okay. It is what I choose to do with it now. My husband always said that in rehab, a special friend who ran the program said, "It's not what you say NO to. It's what you say YES to."

Think about that and mull it over. I like the saying, "That which does not kill me only makes me stronger." It's so fitting as I have always found myself in that type of situation, fortunately and unfortunately. You can do this!

As I continue discussions with an Academy, Emmy, and Tony Award winning producer in Hollywood, I see my life rising above anything I could have ever dreamed. And I KNOW that you, too, are capable of ANYTHING.

And stay tuned for more. There are two more volumes to this East Coast Version of the story. Keep an eye out for the Original Version with true Hawaii locations, coming soon! We are also working on the Wise Marie Merchandise line, including hats, jewelry, T-Shirts, aprons, figurines, and more! Available now, we have stickers for the Wise Marie Series on our website.

Thank you so much for your support!

GLOSSARY OF CHARACTERS

1. **Marie (Wise Marie)**
   - **Description**: The protagonist and narrator of the story, Marie is the alter ego of the author, Natasha Brune. Her life is marked by trauma, addiction, abuse, and eventual self-discovery and growth. Born in 1970 as a result of her mother's affair with "The Italian," Marie's childhood is chaotic, filled with economic hardship, frequent moves, and exposure to substance abuse. As she grows older, Marie rebels against her circumstances, engaging in risky behavior, relationships with older men, and eventually finds a path to recovery and self-improvement.
2. **The Mother**
   - **Description**: A strong-willed woman of Japanese descent. Her name is Haseko. She grew up in a small town in Hawaii. She marries "The Russian," with whom she has four children. She is involved in an affair with "The Italian," leading to Marie's birth. Despite her strictness, she struggles to provide for her family amid economic hardship and a turbulent personal life.
3. **The Russian**
   - **Description**: Marie's mother's husband, a troubled man with severe alcohol problems. Charismatic but deeply flawed, he has worked as a blackjack dealer and photographer. His relationship with Marie's mother is abusive and tumultuous, contributing to the family's instability. Aka Billy.
4. **The Italian**
   - **Description**: A military officer from Queens, New York, with connections to organized crime. He has an affair with Marie's mother that results in Marie's birth. He is portrayed as a charismatic and enigmatic

figure, both a source of attraction and conflict in the family's life. Aka Javier Panterra.

5. **Aunt Carissa**
   - **Description:** Marie's maternal Aunty who took care of the three oldest children when The Mother left The Russian.
6. **Tony Mariani**
   - **Description**: A young Teamster from a crime-connected family, Tony becomes Marie's lover in her teenage years. Their relationship is filled with drug addiction, crime, and eventual betrayal. Despite his flaws, Tony is a key figure in Marie's youth, introducing her to a darker side of life.
7. **Frankie Ferrari**
   - **Description**: Another of Marie's lovers, Frankie is involved in organized crime, with a tragic past that includes witnessing his father's murder. He is emotionally volatile, handsome but troubled, and their relationship is characterized by substance abuse and emotional turmoil.
8. **Jennifer**
   - **Description**: Marie's older sister who takes on a maternal role in the family. She is responsible, hardworking, and eventually moves away to attend college on a scholarship. Her absence leaves Marie more vulnerable to the dangers of her environment.
9. **Peter**
   - **Description**: Marie's older brother, portrayed as a troublemaker involved in drug dealing and criminal activities. He has a problematic relationship with Marie and introduces her to dangerous situations. He is charismatic but reckless, causing significant issues within the family.
10. **Brad**
    - **Description**: Another of Marie's older brothers who is less reckless than Peter but still involved in the chaotic family lifestyle. He plays a supportive role at

times but is largely influenced by his older brother's behavior.

11. **Aaron T**
    - **Description**: A major drug dealer in Vermont who Marie meets when she is sent there to recover from her addiction. Although their relationship is not sexual, he enables Marie's continued drug use, complicating her recovery journey.
12. **Bob Proctor**
    - **Description**: A motivational speaker who plays a pivotal role in Marie's life by inspiring her to continue on her path of sobriety and personal growth after attending one of his seminars in 2015.
13. **Roberta**
    - **Description**: A family friend who tries to help Marie get sober by sending her to Vermont. Despite her well-meaning intentions, her efforts fail as Marie relapses into addiction.
14. **Kate**
    - **Description**: One of Marie's older sisters who works hard to support herself and the family. She often steps in to help Marie and is a more stabilizing influence compared to other family members.
15. **Tiare**
    - **Description:** Peter's girlfriend, and a constant in Marie's life.
16. **Sue Anne**
    - **Description:** The Russian's wife from his third marriage.
17. **Tammy**
    - **Description:** Marie's maternal cousin.
18. **Fiona**
    - **Description:** Marie's maternal cousin.
19. **Erin**
    - **Description:** Kate's daughter, and Marie's niece.
20. **Isabella (Aunt Isabella)**
    - **Description**: A relative of "The Italian" who befriends Marie's mother and becomes her

confidante. She disapproves of "The Russian" and facilitates the affair between Marie's mother and "The Italian."

21. **Tommy Fatone**
    - **Description**: Tony Mariani's cousin who has a brief fling with Marie as an act of revenge against Tony. He is part of the crime network that surrounds Marie.
22. **Candy Panterra**
    - **Description**: The daughter of Javier Panterra. She becomes Marie's friend, and they have a connection through their family histories. She helps Marie confront family secrets.
23. **Javier Panterra**
    - **Description**: A former special ops ranger and U.S. Advisor to the South Vietnam General, Javier had a brief affair with Marie's mother. He denies being Marie's biological father but is connected to the family's past. He is The Italian.
24. **Hiroshi San**
    - **Description**: A figure mentioned in Marie's extended network, likely reflecting the multicultural aspect of her background and the people who influenced her.
25. **Uncle**
    - **Description**: A man Marie's mother dates and eventually marries after leaving "The Russian." He is significantly older and has a complex relationship with Marie, who is instructed to call him "Uncle."
26. **Raymond**
    - **Description**: The son of Marie's stepfather ("Uncle"). He takes care of Marie's mother after her stepfather passes away and plays a supportive role for the family.
27. **Dane**
    - **Description**: A man who breaks into Marie's apartment and attempts to assault her. He is later arrested and becomes a registered sex offender. He represents one of the many dangers Marie faces in her tumultuous life.

28. Davian

- **Description**: A drug dealer Marie meets in Vermont. He is involved in her overdose, highlighting the ongoing cycle of addiction and risky behavior in her life.

29. Mr. B

- **Description:** Drug dealer in and out of Marie's life.

30. Mr. L

- **Description:** The man that Marie is rented to. He is a friend of Mr. B.

31. Jason Panterra

- **Description**: A family friend from Marie's childhood, who later becomes romantically involved with her. He is the brother of Candy Panterra and has connections to Marie's family history. Their brief relationship adds layers to Marie's understanding of her origins.

32. Ronnie

- Marie's ex-boyfriend who she lived with, abuser, phone sex addict, waiter at a classy restaurant in New York City, and professional skateboarder. Their relationship was filled with abuse and terror.

33. Uncle Tony (Tony Abalone)

- **Description**: A relative of Tony Mariani, who also has connections to the crime world. He is mentioned as someone who appears in Marie's life and represents the broader criminal network she is entangled with.

34. Aunty D

- **Description:** Leah's adopted mother.

35. Betsy

- **Description:** The Russian's secretary. She hid The Mother, Jennifer, and Marie when they left The Russian.

36. Elaine

- **Description:** Marie's half-sister from The Italian. She helped Marie try to get her kids back.

37. Max Carrera
- **Description:** Marie's second husband. He is loving and kind to Marie and shares a beautiful life, and a son with Marie.

38. Ace Marinelli
- **Description:** Marie's son, fathered by Rathe. Also disguised as Allen Lee for protection at the hospital.

39. Leah Tiara
- **Description:** Marie's daughter of the Korn from Jesse.

40. Jesse James Jr.
- **Description:** Marie's son and third child. His father is Jesse.

41. Garrett
- **Description:** Marie's son and forth child. His father is Max.

ACKNOWLEDGMENTS

I want to thank all the people who contributed to this story, whether they realize it or not. The patience, dedication, and accuracy that went into the years of this first volume in the series was invaluable.

I'm grateful for the unwavering support from my wonderful family, the publishers, consultants, and my kickass assistant and colleague, who has grown leaps and bounds herself since we met two years ago.

Library of Congress: 2024950973